FACE-OFF

MICHAEL BETCHERMAN

This book was originally published by the Penguin
Group (Canada), (a division of Pearson Canada Inc.)
90 Eglinton Avenue East, Suite 700, Toronto, Ontario,
Canada M4P 2Y3

FOR MY FATHER
IRVING BETCHERMAN
1924-2012

MICHAEL BETCHERMAN is an award-winning screenwriter and author with numerous credits in both documentary and dramatic television. *Face-Off* is his second young adult novel. The first, *Breakaway,* was published by Penguin Canada. It was shortlisted for the John Spray Mystery Award. Betcherman is also the author of two online novels, *The Daughters of Freya* and *Suzanne.* He lives in Toronto with his wife and daughter,

Author's Note:
Some events that are referred to in this book were inspired by the warfare that broke out when the former Republic of Yugoslavia split into several independent countries in the early 1990s. However, Berovia and Maldania are fictional places and do not represent actual countries. The island of Charos does not exist. The Berovian language is a creation of the author.

CHAPTER ONE

Alex stood in front of the mirror. He stared at the stump sticking out of his shoulder, where his right arm used to be. A doctor in a white lab coat was standing behind him. He caught Alex's eye in the mirror. "You'll get used to it," he said with a reassuring smile that didn't reassure Alex one bit. Alex looked at his reflection in the mirror again. He'd never get used to the sight of that. Not in a million years.

The strangest thing was that he couldn't for the life of him remember how he lost his arm. He had both of them at the game the night before. Obviously. He wouldn't have been selected to represent his province in an international hockey tournament if he only had one arm.

He remembered walking out of the arena following Team British Columbia's loss to Team Michigan, his goalie stick in one hand and his hockey bag in the other. He took the bus straight home, unpacked his hockey bag, and went into the kitchen and made himself a grilled cheese and tomato sandwich—a task that required two hands. When he finished eating he went into his mom's office to say good night. It was past ten o'clock but she was working on her computer, as usual. After that he went to his bedroom, played a hockey video game on his computer—another task that required two hands—and went to sleep.

So how did he lose his arm? The doctor was watching him through the mirror. "Shit happens," he said with a shrug.

The doctor's cellphone rang. He appeared not to notice. It rang and rang and rang.

Alex woke up and turned off the alarm clock on his bedside table. He'd been having dreams where he was missing a limb for as long as he could remember. When he was little, the dreams terrified him. He'd wake up screaming, and he wouldn't stop until his mother came into the room and calmed him down. The dreams didn't terrify him anymore. They just made him sad.

"You don't have to be a shrink to figure out why you're having them," his friend Lara said to him once. "You miss your dad."

Alex's dad died when he was one.

Died wasn't really the right word to describe what happened to his father.

He was murdered.

At the time Alex and his parents were living in Berovia, a small country on the island of Charos off the coast of Italy. Berovia was at war with its island neighbor, Maldania. It was the latest in a string of wars between the two countries that went back centuries. The hatred was so deep-rooted that when Alex's mom, a Berovian, married his dad, a Maldan, their families disowned them.

One day, a few months after the war began, Alex and his mother fell ill. His dad went out to get a doctor. He never came back. The next day Alex's mother found out that he'd been killed by Berovian soldiers.

Alex didn't find out how his father died until he was seven. He would never forget the feeling of utter devastation that overwhelmed him when his mother finally told him. "Why did they kill him?" he asked after the shock wore off.

"Because he was a Maldan," his mother answered. "No other reason."

She and Alex came to Vancouver a few months later to live with her brother, Roman. Alex didn't have a single memory of his father. All he had to go on was his name— Darko Petrovic—and a few pictures in an old leather photo album. He often wondered what his life would have been like if his father had lived. It made him angry to know that the men who murdered him would never pay for what they'd done. How could they? Nobody even knew who they were.

CHAPTER TWO

Alex got off the bus in front of the Thunderbird Arena on the campus of the University of British Columbia. For the twentieth time since he woke up that morning he wondered if Coach McAndrew was going to start him in goal for the game against Team Oregon. Alex had played well during the tryouts and he had been disappointed when McAndrew named Eddie Davidson as Team B.C.'s starter. It wasn't just a matter of pride. Scouts from a number of U.S. colleges were in town for the tournament, called the TelCel Cup after its corporate sponsor, and it was Alex's dream to get a scholarship to one of them. It was a golden opportunity to showcase his talent, but first he'd have to get off the bench.

If Davidson had been sharp against Team Michigan in the tournament opener, Alex knew McAndrew would stick with him for tonight's game. But Eddie had let in two shots he should have stopped, and that was the difference in the 4–2 loss. Even though Eddie was a good guy, Alex couldn't help feeling glad that he'd left the door open. The question was whether McAndrew would invite him to walk through it.

Alex was wearing a jacket and tie, despite the July heat wave that was now into its second week. Coach McAndrew said the dress code was mandatory. The players had groaned when he made the announcement but the coach

4

didn't want to hear about it. "You're representing your province," he explained in a tone of voice that made it clear the subject wasn't up for discussion. "You're not going to show up wearing hoodies and unlaced sneakers."

A few of the players complained about McAndrew being "old school," but Alex agreed with the coach. Corny as it sounded, he was proud to have been chosen to represent his province, and wearing a jacket and tie made the event feel more special, more professional, even if it was damn hot.

Alex loosened his tie as he walked into the arena, lugging his bright red Team B.C. hockey bag with his name stenciled on the side. His footsteps echoed on the cement floor. He could hear the crunch of blades and a dull roar from the rink.

"Hey, Alex. Wait up," a voice called out. Kenny Nelson was coming through the entrance. He was the only other player on Team B.C. from the Richmond Cougars, the local rep team Alex played for.

Alex stopped to wait for him. Two middle-aged men were standing by the concession stand. They were both wearing U.S. college jackets, one from the University of Minnesota, one from Boston College.

"We're losing six seniors this year, including our best player," the man in the Boston College jacket said.

Alex's heart started beating a little faster. The two men were college scouts, he realized, and one of them was from the University of Minnesota. *The University of Minnesota!* Alex would be thrilled to get a scholarship to any big-time U.S. college, but Minnesota was the alma mater of his favorite player, the Vancouver Canucks goalie, Lou Roberts, and it was at the top of his wish list.

"I hear Stevens is leaning to Notre Dame 'cause his old

man went there," the man in the Minnesota jacket said. Alex knew he was referring to Eric Stevens, the Team Oregon star. Stevens had broken scoring records everywhere he played, and his size and speed had NHL scouts salivating.

"It ain't over till it's over. We still think we've got a good chance of landing him."

"Big game tonight," Kenny said as he joined Alex.

"It is," Alex answered. Team B.C. had to defeat Team Oregon to keep its hopes of advancing to the medal round alive.

The two of them walked up an aisle that led to the rink. "It's a long way from Triangle Road," Kenny said. Alex nodded. The arena, with its professional scoreboard and 5000 seats, was a big step up from their home arena in Richmond, where a few hundred fans could watch the game provided they didn't mind sitting on each other's laps.

Team Michigan was playing Team Maldania. "How did Maldania get invited to the tournament?" Kenny asked. "They suck." The Maldans had been thrashed 9–0 by Team Oregon in their first game and were down 7–1 to Michigan with less than a minute to go in the game.

"The owner of TelCel was born in Maldania," Alex explained. "He's trying to help them develop their hockey program." The thinking was that Team Maldania would improve by playing against superior competition, and if that was the case then they were certain to get better. The other seven teams in the tournament—four from Canada and three from the States—were head and shoulders above the Maldans.

"I didn't even know they played hockey there," Kenny said.

"Apparently they don't," Alex answered dryly, pointing at the scoreboard.

Team Michigan's left-winger fired a point-blank shot from the slot that the Maldan goalie kicked aside with enough force to send it to the corner, out of reach of the Michigan forwards who were ready to pounce on the rebound. He made it look easy but Alex knew how hard it was to control the puck like that. He noticed that the goalie had a Lou Roberts mask just like he did—white with a lightning bolt on the forehead. And his uniform number was 33, just like Lou, and just like Alex.

A moment later the game ended and Alex and Kenny headed to the locker room. The two scouts were still talking to each other. For the twenty-first time that day, Alex wondered if he was going to start.

He'd find out soon enough. Some coaches liked to keep their goalies in suspense until the last minute. His coach in Peewee would give his pre-game speech and then he would toss the puck to whoever was going to start. If there was a reason he did it that way, Alex had never figured it out. It just seemed cruel.

Thankfully that wasn't McAndrew's style. Before the first game of the tournament he had called Alex into his office and told him that Eddie Davidson would be starting. "It was a hard decision," he said. "You both played well during the tryouts. I'm going with Eddie because he's got more experience than you. It doesn't mean I don't think you can do the job. You showed me what you could do last year," he added. He was talking about last year's semifinals where Alex played brilliantly in Richmond's 2–1 loss to the West Vancouver Lightning, the rep team McAndrew coached. Alex was pretty sure that was the reason McAndrew invited him to try out for Team B.C.

"Coach wants to see you," Charlie Boyle, the assistant coach, said to Alex as soon as he walked into the locker room. *Here we go again*, Alex thought, nervously snapping the rubber band he wore around his left wrist.

The door to McAndrew's office was open. "You wanted to see me, Coach?" Alex asked, steeling himself for bad news.

"I'm going with you tonight," McAndrew said, running a hand through his thinning red hair.

"I under …" *I understand*, Alex was about to say until his brain caught up to McAndrew's words. *Holy shit. I'm starting*. He could feel a smile spread across his face. The coach was looking at him, waiting for him to say something. "Thank you," Alex said.

"Just play your game and you'll be fine."

"Thank you," Alex said again. The reality of the situation hit him before he was out of the coach's office. He was the starting goalie in an international hockey tournament, in a must-win game against a powerful opponent led by the best seventeen-year-old hockey player in the universe. His stomach was always churning before a game but now it went into overdrive. *Don't screw up*, the Voice warned.

The Voice was a negative inner voice that had played on Alex's insecurities for as long as he could remember. Even when he played well, the Voice was there, lurking in the background, whispering that the Alex who played well was an impostor. Alex knew his biggest problem was his lack of self-confidence. "You can't be solid between the pipes if you're not solid between the ears," was the way one of the coaches at goalie camp put it. *Problem is*, the Voice piped up, *you're not solid between the ears*.

Alex sat down at his locker, took off his clothes, and

began to put on his equipment in the same order he always did. Goalies tended to be superstitious and he was no exception. Jock, underwear, pants, left skate, right skate, left pad, right pad, chest protector, Team B.C. jersey.

He knew his teammates were also feeling the pressure, but it was different for a goalie. Anybody who knew anything about hockey knew that the goalie was under more pressure than anyone else on the team. If a position player made a mistake that gave the opponent a scoring opportunity, the goalie could always bail him out with a good save. When a goalie made a mistake it showed up on the scoreboard.

He wondered why on earth he ever decided to become a goalie. It was a question he asked himself before every game. But he knew the answer. It was the high he felt when he was on his game, the belief that he was invincible, that nobody could put the puck by him. It was seeing his teammates play with more confidence because they knew they could count on him to keep the other team off the score sheet; it was seeing his opponents play hesitantly because they felt like they were shooting the puck at a brick wall. "You have to want to be a hero if you're going to be a goalie," was the way Lou Roberts put it in an article Alex once read.

The flip side of being a hero was being the goat, letting in a goal that cost your team the game. That was every goalie's fear, and Alex was no exception, which was why it felt like somebody was operating a jackhammer in his stomach.

Everybody went silent as Coach McAndrew came out of his office and made his way to the center of the room.

"Listen up," he said. "I know we have to win tonight if we're going to move on, but you've got to put that out of your mind and stay in the present. If we want to win we've got to do it one shift at a time. We've got to finish our checks and we've got to come up with the puck every time we go into the corner. We're representing our province, men. Let's make them proud of us. Bring it in."

The team gathered around the coach. "One. Two. Three. Defense," the team roared and stormed out of the locker room.

"Oh Canada, we stand on guard for thee."

Alex stood on the blue line beside the rest of his teammates as the arena echoed with the last notes of the national anthem. There had to be at least three thousand people in the stands, by far the biggest crowd he had ever played in front of. A powerful feeling of pride at playing for his province swept over him. The pride was accompanied by a sense of what was at stake. *This is the biggest game of your life*, the Voice reminded Alex, just in case he'd forgotten.

Alex glanced at the U.S. team standing at the other blue line. He didn't need a program to identify Eric Stevens. He was a head taller than everybody else. And he looked mean. Real mean.

Alex put on his Lou Roberts goalie mask and skated down to Team B.C.'s end of the ice. His teammates came by one-by-one and tapped him on his pads with their sticks to wish him luck. He skated from side to side, scraping the ice in the crease. He took a few deep breaths to calm himself, but he knew the butterflies in his stomach would keep fluttering until he faced his first shot.

Stick on the ice. Square up to the shooter. Stand your ground, he said to himself, steadying himself with the mantra he repeated before every game.

The first shot wasn't long in coming. Twenty seconds into the game Eric Stevens roared down the left wing, blew past Don Herron like he was standing still, and fired a bullet at the top corner that Alex deflected with his blocker at the last moment. *Bring it on*, Alex thought, as the self-doubt flowed out of his body and the confidence flowed in.

Five minutes later Kenny Nelson steered a rebound past the U.S. goalie to give B.C. a 1–0 lead. Three minutes later the home team scored again. Team Oregon dominated the second period but Alex kept them at bay. Early in the third, Eric Stevens finally managed to beat Alex with a shot from the slot that he could only wave at. The Americans kept the pressure up but they couldn't put the puck past Alex. With ninety seconds left, Team Oregon pulled their goalie. The Oregon players buzzed around the B.C. goal like a swarm of angry bees, firing shots from every angle in a desperate attempt to notch the equalizer, but Alex was up to the task.

When the final buzzer sounded, his teammates jumped over the boards and raced to the goal to congratulate him. Everybody knew that his heroics had saved the day.

The celebration continued in the locker room, but the conversation soon turned to Team Oregon's game against Michigan the following day. The eight teams in the tournament were divided into two four-team divisions. Only two teams in each division advanced to the medal round. B.C. was in the same division as Michigan, Oregon, and Maldania. Assuming B.C. beat Maldania, which was pretty much a given, Michigan would have to defeat Oregon in order for Alex and his teammates to move on.

Everyone quieted down when Coach McAndrew came into the room. "Nice win, men," he said. "You guys should be proud of yourselves. You beat a heckuva hockey team tonight."

"You were awesome, man," Len Dawson said to Alex after McAndrew left the room. "We wouldn't have won without you." The other players nodded in agreement. Alex kept his head down but inside he was sky high. Lou Roberts had it right. "You have to want to be a hero if you're going to be a goalie."

CHAPTER THREE

"See you tomorrow, Kenny," Alex said as they came out of the locker room.

"Later. Great game, man."

Alex walked to the concession stand. The girl behind the counter was cute. She glanced at Alex's Team B.C. bag. "Congratulations," she said. "You guys were fantastic."

"Thanks." The girl gave Alex an encouraging smile. He smiled back at her, but as usual, he couldn't think of anything to say.

"What can I get you?" she asked after a few seconds.

"Coke. No ice." *Where did you learn to be so smooth?* the Voice asked sarcastically.

"Great game, Alex. You were amazing." Lara walked beside him and gave him a quick hug.

"Thanks. I thought you were working today." Alex and Lara both had summer jobs at his uncle's travel agency.

"Things were slow so Uncle Roman let me leave early." Lara called Roman *uncle* even though he was actually her dad's cousin by marriage.

"You look sharp," Lara said, taking in his jacket and tie. "Your mommy take you shopping?"

"Ha, ha."

The girl at the concession stand handed him his Coke.

"You shouldn't be drinking that stuff," Lara said. "Do you know how much sugar there is in it?"

"You gonna tell my mommy?"

Lara laughed. Alex wished he could be as loose with other girls as he was with her. Like with Jenna. Jenna worked at a café near the travel agency. Roman sent him there every day on an espresso run, and every time he went he was determined to ask her out, but he could never pull the trigger. He was pretty sure she liked him, she always greeted him with a big smile, but he hadn't been able to say much more than "two espressos, please," let alone ask her out.

It was different with Lara. He'd known her since they were little kids. He didn't feel he had to impress her.

"I gotta pee," Lara said. He watched her walk toward the washroom in her tight-fitting jeans. *She's definitely not a little kid anymore*, he thought. It felt a little strange to be thinking of Lara that way, but they'd been working side-by-side at the travel agency every day for the past month and it wasn't the first time he'd had the thought. Across the hallway a guy in a Team Maldania jacket was watching her walk away as well. From the way he was looking at her, it was clear he didn't think she was a little kid either.

"Pila voja," he said to Alex after Lara disappeared into the washroom. *Pretty girl.*

Alex nodded. He wondered why the guy was speaking to him in Berovian—although since he was a Maldan he would have said he was speaking Maldanian. Maldans and Berovians spoke the same language—they just called it by different names. Then he realized the guy must have seen his name on his hockey bag. Petrovic was a dead giveaway, the Berovian equivalent of Smith or Jones.

"Ready?" Lara asked when she came out of the washroom. Alex picked up his hockey bag and he and Lara headed off. The Maldan gave him a curious look.

14

"*Vo dinya,*" Alex said. *Goodbye.* It was one of the few things he could say in Berovian, although he still understood the language. He and his mother had spoken Berovian until they moved out of Roman's house a few years after they arrived in Vancouver, when they could afford a place of their own. After that they only spoke English. His mom insisted on it. She said it was important if he was going to do well in school.

The University of Minnesota scout was standing by the exit. He glanced at Alex's name on his hockey bag. "That was a heck of a performance, son," he said.

"Thanks," Alex said, trying not to sound too excited even though his insides were bursting.

The scout put out his hand. Alex shook it. "Bill Henry. University of Minnesota."

"Alex Petrovic."

"What grade are you in, Alex?"

"Going into grade twelve."

"Are you planning to go to university?"

"Yes, sir."

"You going to stay here in Canada?"

"Not necessarily. I guess it depends on whether I get any offers to go to the States."

"That shouldn't be a problem, son. Not if that's the way you normally play. You got some serious game."

You got some serious game. The words sent a chill up Alex's spine.

"How cool was that?" Lara said after the scout walked away. "You must be flying." She knew how much Alex wanted to go to Minnesota.

"It's no big deal," Alex said nonchalantly.

"No big deal," Lara repeated with a smile that told him he wasn't fooling her for a minute.

CHAPTER FOUR

Alex was awakened the next morning by another one of his dreams. This time he was missing a leg, which was particularly inconvenient because he was playing goal at the time. The dream faded away as soon as he sat up. All he could remember was that everybody on the other team was wearing a Lou Roberts goalie mask.

The sun was streaming into his bedroom. It was only a quarter to eight, but according to the thermometer outside his window the temperature had already hit seventy degrees. It was going to be another scorcher.

There was no point trying to go back to sleep. He had to get up at eight o'clock in order to get to the travel agency by nine. He got out of bed and did his push-ups and sit-ups. He'd started doing them a little over three years ago and he hadn't missed a single day since, except when he had his appendix out. When he started he could only do twenty-five push-ups and fifty sit-ups, but now he was up to eighty-five push-ups and one hundred and fifty sit-ups.

When he finished he stood in front of the mirror and checked out his physique. The three small scars from his appendectomy were still visible above the waistband of his boxers. The doctor said it would take a few years for them to completely disappear. He flexed in front of the mirror, as if he were posing for a body-building competition. His arms were definitely getting bigger but they weren't exactly what you'd call pipes. He wished he wasn't so skinny but he couldn't put on any weight no matter how much he ate.

Team B.C. was playing Maldania later that day. On his way downstairs Alex tapped the full-size poster of Lou Roberts that was taped to his bedroom door for good luck, something he always did on game day. Lou was crouched in goal, his eyes—one brown and one green—staring out of his goalie mask with an intensity that always caught Alex's attention.

Alex had bought the poster at a Canucks game several years earlier and had waited outside the locker room after the game so Lou could sign it. When he told Lou he was a goalie, too—kind of cheesy, he had to admit, but hey, he was only twelve at the time—Lou wrote "To a member of the clan" on the bottom of the poster. That's when Lou officially became his favorite player.

He remembered that the Team Maldania goalie had a Lou Roberts mask, too. Maybe that explained his dream, he thought, although he was more concerned with Team Oregon's game against Team Michigan than with his own against Maldania. The Maldans were so bad that Team B.C. would beat them even if Alex really did have only one leg.

The article in *The Vancouver Sun* about the game the night before was short, but it was sweet. "Team Oregon dominated the play but the Americans were turned back time and again by Team B.C.'s goalie, Alex Petrovic, whose outstanding play allowed the home team to escape with a 2–1 win."

A heckuva way to start the day, Alex thought as he put the newspaper on the kitchen table and stood up to make his breakfast. He cracked three eggs into a bowl, added a little milk, and whisked the mixture until it was a uniform color.

He took a few anchovies out of a jar on the counter, chopped them up, and scraped them into the bowl. Then he put two pieces of bread in the toaster and poured the eggs into a frying pan, stirring them gently with a spoon.

He'd been making a lot of his own breakfasts since he was ten, and a lot of his dinners, too. It had started out as a necessity—his mother usually left early in the morning for work and often didn't get home until late at night—but now he enjoyed it.

"There's nothing sexier than a man who knows his way around a kitchen," Lara joked one time when he made her dinner while they were working on a school project. He wouldn't serve her until she promised not to tell any of his teammates on the Richmond Cougars. That was the kind of thing a jerk like Mike Leonard would grab hold of and never let go. Leonard didn't need much of a reason to make someone's life miserable, and finding out that Alex liked to cook would more than do the trick.

When the scrambled eggs were ready, Alex spooned them onto a plate and spread some peanut butter and grape jelly on his toast. He was about to sit down when his mom came into the kitchen.

"Morning, Anna." He bent over and gave her a kiss. He was always surprised at how small she was. In his mind's eye she was a lot taller than five foot one.

"Morning, dude," she said.

She started calling him dude a few years ago, when he started calling her Anna. It had started out as a joke but the names had stuck.

"Are you coming home before your game tonight?" she asked.

"No. I'm going to the arena straight from the travel agency."

"I'll try to make it but I'm not sure I'll be able to. It depends how long my meeting with the contractor lasts." Anna owned three health food stores in the Lower Mainland and was about to open a fourth in Langley.

"That's okay," Alex said. "It's not going to be much of a game."

"Is Maldania that bad?"

"Worse."

Work kept his mother so busy that she rarely made it to his games. It used to bother him when he was a kid. He'd come out of the locker room after the game and have to stand there by himself while his teammates were being congratulated by their parents. "I'm as disappointed as you are," Anna told him once when he was upset because she couldn't come to a playoff game. "One of the joys of being a parent is sharing the important moments in your child's life. It kills me to miss out on that." It was obvious once she said it, but Alex had never looked at things that way. It was the last time he ever brought up the subject.

He knew he wouldn't have been able to play hockey if Anna hadn't worked so hard. It was an expensive sport. Equipment, especially goalie equipment, didn't come cheap. Then there were the registration fees and travel expenses when he had to go out of town to a tournament. They were financially secure now, but that hadn't always been the case. He knew his mother had gone without things she wanted for herself so that he could play hockey. Yet she had never complained about the cost. She always made sure he had what he needed.

"I've got to run," Anna said, glancing at her watch. "I have interviews all morning for the manager's job at the store in Abbotsford."

"You should eat something first," he said.

"I'm the parent, remember?" she said.

"I can make you eggs. It will only take a couple of minutes." For someone who was in the health food business, his mother had terrible eating habits.

"I'll grab something on the way," Anna said, walking out of the kitchen and into the hallway.

Alex looked at her as she stood in front of the mirror applying her lipstick. His mother wasn't an unhappy person, but there was a heaviness to her that she could never seem to shed, as if she were carrying an invisible weight on her shoulders. That was only natural, Alex thought. She'd been through a lot.

He wondered if she was lonely. There had been a few boyfriends over the years, but none of them had lasted. Part of the reason was that work kept her so busy that she had no time for a social life. But Alex thought the main reason was that no relationship could measure up to what she had with his father. One thing for sure, the two of them must have really loved each other to get married in the first place.

"The fact that we were two human beings who loved each other didn't matter to my parents," Anna told him once. "I could have been a murderer and they would have stuck by me. But marrying a Maldan, that was something they couldn't forgive."

Anna saw him looking at her in the mirror. She looked at her watch. "I gotta scoot," she said. "Later, dude."

CHAPTER FIVE

The bus ride to the travel agency normally took twenty minutes, but traffic was unusually light so Alex arrived early. Roman was the only other person there.

"I need you to take a look at my computer," he said. "It's not working."

"Did you try restarting it?" Alex asked as they walked into his uncle's office.

"I keep forgetting to do that," Roman said. He was useless when it came to computers. "That was quite a write-up you got in the paper," he said enthusiastically as Alex sat down at his desk.

"It was nice," Alex said calmly as he restarted the computer.

"Nice?" Roman scoffed. "It was fantastic. Who do you play tonight?"

"Team Maldania."

"Tak voi guz," he said gruffly, a scowl appearing on his face. *Kick their ass.* Even though Roman had been in Vancouver for nearly thirty years, he considered himself Berovian first and Canadian a distant second. All his friends were from Berovia—Anna called them the Berovian Mafia—and he talked about the war with Maldania as if he'd been in it despite the fact that he left Berovia years before it started.

"We'll do our best ... That should do it," Alex said

after he confirmed that the computer was working.

Lara was on the phone when Alex got back to his desk. "I'll see if Mr. Kuchar is free to talk to you." She pushed the hold button and then pushed another button to connect with Roman. "Another cranky client for you, Uncle Roman. He wants a partial refund because his return flight was delayed," she said, rolling her eyes at Alex. It was amazing how many customers complained about things that were beyond the travel agency's control, as if using it should be a guarantee that every meal would be cooked to perfection and all the arrangements would run like clockwork.

Just then, Greta, the agency's travel consultant, came through the front door. She was wearing a tight-fitting dress that revealed every curve of her outstanding body. "Can you do me a favor, sweetie?" she asked Alex. "Find out what the visa requirements to Zambia are."

"I'll get right on it," Alex said, trying not to stare at her chest.

"Thanks." She ruffled his hair affectionately and walked to her desk, hips swiveling. Alex watched her leave.

"Careful your jaw doesn't hit the floor," Lara said. She walked to the filing cabinet and put a folder away.

"That obvious, huh?"

Greta put her purse on her desk and continued down the hallway toward the washroom.

"Can you do me a favor, sweetie?" Lara said, mocking Greta. Then she made a gagging motion, putting her fingers in her mouth. Alex laughed. "She is personally setting women back fifty years," Lara said.

"It's disgraceful," Alex said, craning his head in Greta's direction in an exaggerated motion, his eyes riveted on her butt.

Lara laughed. "What time is your game tonight?" she asked.

"Six o'clock. You coming?"

"Can't make it."

"Seeing the nerd?"

"If you mean Jason," she said sharply, "yes. And he's not a nerd."

"You're right," Alex said. "He's a jerk, not a nerd." He regretted saying the words as soon as they left his mouth.

"You're the jerk," Lara said angrily.

"Sorry," Alex said. Lara stared at him. "That was out of line." Lara kept staring. "Way out of line."

Lara nodded, finally accepting his apology. Then she spun around, shooting her leg out in a ninja kick that missed his head by a few carefully calculated inches. "Just don't let it happen again, Petrovic," she said. "Or I'm going to have to mess you up."

Alex laughed, but the truth was that Lara probably could mess him up even though she was barely half his size. She was into muay Thai—kickboxing, most people called it—and she was good enough to compete on a provincial level. Alex went to most of her fights, and he was always shocked by the transformation that came over her the minute she put on her gloves and entered the ring. The friendly smile and the warm gaze vanished, replaced by hard eyes and tight-set lips. She was absolutely fearless. He'd seen her get knocked on her ass with blows that he was sure would keep her down for the count, but she'd be back up on her feet in a few seconds with a look of fury on her face that usually spelled disaster for her unfortunate opponent.

Alex knew he shouldn't have said anything about Jason but he couldn't help himself. The guy *was* a jerk. He could be fun, and he was good-looking, Alex grudgingly admitted, but he didn't treat Lara with the respect she deserved. Even though she was a hundred times smarter than he was, he acted like her opinions didn't count.

He wondered if they were having sex. They probably were, he thought. Everybody seemed to be having sex these days. *Everybody except you*, the Voice chimed in. Alex had never had sex. That was his deep dark secret, something he had never told a living soul, and never would. He'd come close with Aimee a few weeks ago, just after school ended. It was the last time they saw each other before she moved to Rochester. They'd been going out for a few months by then and things were getting hot and heavy. He was pretty sure she wanted to do it that last night, but for some reason he just couldn't make his move.

Now Aimee was in Rochester and he was still a virgin. *A virgin*. He hated the freakin' word. He knew he wasn't the only seventeen-year-old in the world who'd never had sex, but it sure seemed like it. Getting laid—how often and with how many girls—was a prime topic of conversation in the locker room. Not all of the guys bragged about the girls they were sleeping with, but the ones who didn't brag about it made sure to drop a comment or two that let everybody know they were getting some. He'd done it himself. He couldn't be the only one who was lying. Could he?

At four o'clock Alex went into Roman's office to tell him that he had to leave for his game. Roman was talking to his marketing manager, Tomas Radich.

"Maria's insisting we send Lina to private school," Tomas was saying. "You know how much that costs?"

"Fifteen thousand?" Roman suggested.

"Try twenty-five," Tomas said. He turned to Alex. "I hear you played a great game yesterday."

"It was a good win," he said automatically, as if he were being interviewed on TV, where it was considered bad form to talk about yourself.

"He's going to be the next Mike Barkich," Roman said.

Yeah, right, Alex thought. Mike Barkich was the only Berovian to ever play in the NHL, but no matter what Roman might think, Alex knew he wasn't going to be the second. Like any kid who'd ever laced up a pair of skates, he had fantasized about playing in the NHL, but he'd played enough hockey by now to know that wasn't going to happen. It wasn't a lack of confidence that made him reach this conclusion; it was a fact. Only sixty men in the entire world got to play goal in the NHL—two for each of the thirty teams—and even though Alex knew he was good, maybe even better than he thought, he knew he wasn't close to being good enough to become a member of that club. But he might just be good enough to get a scholarship to the University of Minnesota. *And that would be just fine with me*, he thought.

"Who do you play next?" Tomas asked.

"Maldania."

"Kick their ass," Tomas ordered. Tomas was a charter member of the Berovian Mafia. He was even more crazed about the war than Roman was.

"We'll do our best," Alex said. But beating Maldania wasn't the problem. The question was whether Michigan would beat Oregon so that B.C. would move on to the medal round.

CHAPTER SIX

"Don't make the mistake of taking these guys for granted," McAndrew cautioned in the locker room before the game. "Divac isn't going to give up any easy ones," he said, referring to Team Maldania's goalie, Stefan Divac, "so we've got to keep up the pressure for all sixty minutes."

McAndrew was right about Divac. Alex remembered how well he'd played at the end of the game against Team Michigan. He and his teammates knew that a hot goalie could win a game all by himself, but everybody in the locker room, including McAndrew, knew that there was no way Maldania was going to beat them, no matter how well Divac played.

"Don't get distracted wondering whether Michigan is going to beat Oregon," the coach continued, knowing that was exactly what was on everybody's mind. "We can't do anything about that. We need to win tonight to give ourselves a chance to move on. So let's go out there and take care of business."

Team B.C. took care of business, as ordered. Stefan Divac was magnificent, but the talent gulf between the teams was too wide and B.C. kept its medal hopes alive with a 5–0 victory.

Alex spent most of the game leaning against the crossbar while his teammates mercilessly bombarded

Divac. The Maldan goalie made a dozen saves Alex would have been proud to feature on his highlight reel. Team Maldania managed to send just a handful of shots Alex's way and only one was even remotely testing: a quick wrist shot from the wing that Alex played perfectly by coming out of his net to cut off the angle. It was the easiest shutout he ever had.

Could have played this one in my street clothes, he thought as his teammates piled over the boards to congratulate him. He glanced at Anna, who was sitting behind the team bench. She'd been able to make it after all. She gave him a thumbs-up and, making a gesture to indicate that she'd meet him outside the locker room, headed for the exit.

It's up to Team Michigan now, Alex thought as he took off his mask and skated to center ice for the traditional post-game handshake. He was so preoccupied with thoughts of the upcoming Oregon–Michigan matchup that he had shaken hands with half the Maldan players before it registered that they were all looking at him strangely.

He realized why when he reached the end of the line and found himself face-to-face with Stefan Divac.

He could have been looking in the mirror. Stefan Divac looked exactly like him, right down to the mole under his left eye. Neither of them said a word. They just stared at each other for a moment, wide-eyed and uncomprehending, before skating away. When Alex reached his bench, he turned and looked across the ice. Stefan was standing by the Maldan bench, looking back at him. He held up his Lou Roberts mask. Alex did the same. Then they both turned and walked off the ice.

"You don't have a twin brother you never told me about, do you?" Kenny Nelson joked when Alex walked into the locker room.

Alex was asking himself the same question, but he wasn't joking. He didn't know what to think. His gut was telling him that Stefan Divac was his twin brother even though his brain was telling him that was impossible. How could he have a brother he knew nothing about? And if they were brothers, his last name would be Petrovic, not Divac, wouldn't it?

"Listen up," Charlie Boyle shouted. The room went quiet. Boyle waved a stack of tickets. "I've got tickets for anyone who wants to see the Michigan–Oregon game."

The other players all gathered around Boyle but Alex's thoughts were elsewhere. He spotted a copy of the tournament program lying on the floor. He picked it up and turned to the page with Team Maldania's roster. Each player's birth date and place of birth were listed beside his name. The players were listed in alphabetical order. Stefan Divac was the second name on the list. It didn't make any sense, but Alex was suddenly positive he knew what he would see in the other columns. Sarno, Berovia. February 11. Same as him.

He was wrong. Stefan was born in Sarno all right, but his birthday was January 27, not February 11. Alex took a second look to make sure his eyes weren't playing tricks on him. They weren't. He and Stefan were born on different days. They couldn't be brothers. He stared at the program blankly. He felt as if the wind had been knocked out of him.

"Are you okay?" Kenny asked.

"Fine," Alex said. But he wasn't fine. Not even close.

Stefan was standing in the hallway when Alex came out of the locker room. Alex was vaguely aware that the other people waiting outside the locker room were staring at them. The stunned look on Stefan's face made it clear that he was as confused and overwhelmed as Alex was.

"I'm Stefan," he said finally. He spoke with a heavy accent.

"Alex."

They solemnly shook hands, their eyes not leaving each other's face. As soon as their hands touched, Alex felt as if a bolt of electricity had flowed into him, as if a current that had been switched off had been turned back on. He had the overpowering feeling that they had met before, even though he knew that couldn't possibly be true.

"Do you speak English?" Alex asked.

"Yeah. Everybody in Maldania does. We take it in school from grade one."

"You speak really well."

Stefan shrugged. *I can't believe how much he looks like me*, Alex thought. "This is freaky," he said.

"Freaky?" Stefan asked.

"Strange. Really strange. Like …" Alex made a *who-oo-oo* sound, like in a horror movie.

"Freaky," Stefan agreed.

"The moment I saw you I was positive we were twins. Then I saw that we had different birthdays."

"How do you know my birthday?" Stefan asked.

Alex opened the program to the Team Maldania page and handed it to Stefan. He pointed to Stefan's January 27 birthdate. "I was born on February 11," Alex said.

"January 27 isn't my real birthday," Stefan said. "I'm adopted. That's the date my dad got me from the orphanage. The doctor told him I was around a year old so he chose it as my birthday. I don't know my real birthday."

Alex could feel his heart start to beat faster. "I was born in Sarno, too," he said. He noticed that Stefan had a rubber band on his left wrist.

Alex held up his left wrist.

"Freaky," Stefan said.

Alex felt … he didn't know how he felt. He and Stefan were born in the same town. They were the same age. They looked exactly alike. It all added up to the two of them being twins, but if he had a brother, why didn't Anna tell him? He was trying to solve that puzzle when he looked over Stefan's shoulder and saw a middle-aged man with black hair and bushy eyebrows walking toward him. He was looking straight at Alex and he had a big smile on his face.

"Barod ragi, sin," the man said to Alex. *Good game, son.* At the sound of his voice, Stefan turned around to face him. The man's eyes moved between the two boys. Then he held his hands out as if to say, *What's going on?*

"This is Alex," Stefan said in Berovian, "the B.C. goalie. This is my dad, Boris," he said to Alex. He turned back to Boris. "Alex was born in Sarno."

"Sarno," Boris repeated. He said something to Stefan but Alex wasn't listening. He saw his mother walk toward him. Stefan turned, following Alex's gaze. As soon as Anna saw Stefan, she stopped in her tracks. The blood drained out of her face, as if she'd seen a ghost. Then she fainted dead away.

CHAPTER SEVEN

Alex hovered over his mother, his emotions ping-ponging between concern for his mom and shock at the realization that he had a twin brother. Anna's reaction when she saw Stefan had eliminated all doubt about that. *Why didn't Mom tell me?* The question kept reverberating inside his head, as if it was on an endless loop.

A wave of relief washed over him when his mother finally opened her eyes.

Stefan. Mija Stefan ... Milo damse marte," she said, reverting to her mother tongue. *Stefan. My Stefan. I thought you were dead.* She sat up and took Stefan's face in her two hands, as if she had to touch him to prove she wasn't dreaming. "I thought you were dead," she repeated, this time in English.

Why did she think he was dead? Alex felt hopelessly confused, and judging by the looks on everyone else's face, he wasn't the only one.

It didn't take long to sort things out. It was like a jigsaw puzzle where Anna had some of the pieces and Boris had the others. Between them they were able to put the puzzle together.

The story Anna had told Alex was true, as far as it went. The two of them had been ill and his father had gone to get the doctor. She'd just omitted one little detail—the fact that Alex had a twin brother. "Darko had to take

Stefan with him because I was too sick to take care of him," she said. "I knew something bad happened when they didn't come back. The next day I learned that Darko had been killed ..." She touched Stefan's face. "I thought you ..." She couldn't complete the sentence. She took a deep breath to compose herself and then looked at Boris. "Do you know how he ended up at the orphanage?"

"The people there told me that a woman brought him but they didn't know who she was," Boris said. "He'd already been there for a few days."

"Why did you decide to adopt him?" Anna asked.

Boris shrugged. "My wife and I couldn't have children and there were all these kids with nobody to take care of them." He shrugged, as if anybody would have done the same thing.

"Where's your wife now?"

"She was killed in a bombing raid a few weeks after we got to Maldania."

"I'm so sorry," Anna said. Boris shrugged again. "And you never remarried?"

Boris shook his head. "After the war I put a notice in the Sarno newspapers with Stefan's picture and the details of what happened. When nobody answered it, I adopted him."

"We were already in Canada by then ... One thing I don't understand," she went on. "How did you know his name was Stefan?"

"I didn't. I named him after my father."

Anna looked at Stefan mournfully. "All these years, all these years." A tear trickled down her cheek. She hugged Stefan, burying her head in his chest.

Stefan looked at Alex over Anna's head. As their eyes met, Alex saw the same look of shock and disbelief on his brother's face that he imagined was pasted on his. And he knew his brother felt the same bittersweet emotions he was feeling: the sweetness of reuniting with the brother he never knew he had, and the bitterness that came from knowing that all those years were lost forever.

They drove straight from the arena to the hotel where Team Maldania was staying. Alex and Stefan talked the entire time. It felt bizarre, at first, to hear his mirror image speaking English with a Berovian accent. It was as if he and Stefan had lived all those years in parallel universes that had somehow merged into one. But the strangeness quickly wore off, and Alex soon felt as if he and his brother were merely catching up with each other after a long separation.

When they arrived at the hotel, Boris and Stefan took the elevator up to their rooms to get their luggage. They were moving in with Anna and Alex instead of going on the week-long tour of the province that the owner of TelCel had arranged for the Maldanian contingent.

"I can't believe he's alive," Anna said. She was talking more to herself than to Alex.

"Why didn't you tell me I had a brother?" Alex asked accusingly.

The question jolted his mother out of her reverie. She turned to face him. "I thought it was kinder not to," she said.

"Kinder? How was it kinder?"

"Remember, I thought Stefan was dead. I thought he'd been murdered just like your father. What good would it have done to tell you?"

"Because it was the truth. Because then I would have understood why I felt the way I did, why I always felt that something was missing, why I kept having the dreams."

"I was afraid it would only make the dreams worse."

"You should have told me," he said.

Anna reached out and touched his cheek. He sat frozen in his chair. "Maybe it was a mistake," she said, her voice cracking. "Maybe I should have told you. I don't know. I did what I thought was best."

"You should have told me," he repeated, this time in a softer voice. "Maybe not when I was a kid, but you should have told me when I got older. I had the right to know the truth."

"This is a picture of your father and me a couple of weeks after we met." Anna was sitting on the living-room couch between Alex and Stefan, holding a worn leather photo album on her lap. Boris had gone up to his room after dinner. He said he was tired but Alex knew he wanted to give Stefan a chance to be alone with his mother and his brother.

"How old were you?" Stefan asked. Alex studied his brother's face as he looked at the photo. It was unreal. To think that all these years he had a twin brother he knew nothing about. It was incredible. Absolutely incredible. Stefan glanced at him. Alex could tell his brother was having as much trouble wrapping his mind around it as he was. *I can't believe Mom never told me*, he thought.

"I was eighteen. He was twenty," Anna said. "I haven't looked at these pictures in years. I'd forgotten how much you boys look like him."

"How did you meet?" Stefan asked. Alex knew the story but it had been a while since he'd heard it and he was happy to hear it again.

"It was during the summer holidays. I went to the beach with a few of my girlfriends. Your father was there.

He was very shy. I knew he was looking at me, but every time I caught his eye he looked away. Finally, just as we were about to leave, he came over and said hello. We saw each other every day after that for the rest of the summer. I knew my father would go crazy if he found out I was seeing a Maldan, so we had to meet in secret.

"At first that made it more exciting, but after a while all the lying began to wear us down. One day, about a year later, Darko said he'd had enough. He came to the house and told my father that he loved me and wanted to marry me. My dad was a big man, a lot bigger than Darko, and when he got angry it was a scary sight. He told Darko to go away and said he would kill him if he ever came back. Darko didn't back down. He told my father to go ahead and kill him because he wasn't going to give me up. My father ordered me to make a choice: him or Darko.

"I walked out the door with nothing but the clothes on my back. I wrote my parents to tell them where we were living, but they didn't answer. As far as they were concerned, I didn't exist. I never spoke to them again. They both died a few years after we came to Canada." She stared off into space.

"Everyone thought I came here to get away from the memories," she said a few seconds later, "but that wasn't the reason. I came to get away from the hatred. I couldn't stand it anymore. It's insane. We look the same, we eat the same foods, we speak the same language. The rest of the world can't tell us apart, but you put a Maldan in the same room with a Berovian and the odds are they'll be at each other's throats within a few minutes."

She turned to the next page in the photo album. "This is the apartment we were living in when you two were born," she said. She continued flipping the pages. There were a lot of baby pictures. Alex had always assumed they were of him but now he wasn't so sure.

"Some of those are of Stefan, aren't they?" he asked. Anna nodded.

"Did you keep any pictures of Alex and me?" Stefan asked. Alex was wondering the same thing.

Anna looked through the album until she found a photo of Darko sitting on a couch holding a baby in his lap. "That's you," she said to Stefan. She turned a few more pages and found a photo of herself on the same couch, also holding a baby on her lap. She turned to Alex. "And that's you."

"You can tell I'm older," Stefan joked. He was born ten minutes before Alex.

Anna took the two photos out of the album and put them side-by-side. They were a perfect fit.

CHAPTER EIGHT

Alex woke up the next day feeling, maybe for the first time ever, that all was right with the world. He finally understood why he had his dreams, and he knew with absolute certainty that he would never have one again. He had found his missing limb.

He and Stefan had stayed up talking until the early hours of the morning. Even though they had known each other for less than twenty-four hours, he felt a connection with his brother that he had never felt with another human being. *It's no wonder*, he thought. He and Stefan had spent nine months entangled in their mother's womb, just the two of them, alone in a private universe where nobody else existed.

It wasn't long before they discovered that their similarities didn't end with the fact that they were both goalies, that Lou Roberts was their favorite player, and that they both wore rubber bands around their left wrist. They also used the same brand of toothpaste, were big Bruce Springsteen fans, and had pet snakes when they were seven.

None of that surprised Alex. When he was in grade ten he did a science project on identical twins. He remembered reading about two brothers who met at the age of thirty-nine after having been separated at birth. Both had been named James by their adoptive parents. Each had been married twice, the first time to women named Linda and then to ones named Betty. Their sons had the same names. They smoked the same cigarettes, drank the same beer, and drove the same model of car.

And that was just one story. There were plenty of others that were just as amazing. Alex was pretty sure he and Stefan would find other things to add to their list.

He got out of bed and did his push-ups and sit-ups. After he put on his jeans and a T-shirt, he walked down the hall and knocked on the door to his mom's office, where Stefan had slept on the pullout couch.

"Come in," Stefan called. He was doing push-ups, wearing only a pair of boxers. "Almost done," he grunted.

Alex smiled to himself and mentally made an addition to the list. Stefan's back muscles expanded and contracted with each push-up. Alex noticed, with a twinge of envy, that his brother was more muscular than he was.

Stefan's guitar was on the couch. Alex idly plucked a few strings while Stefan finished his push-ups. When Stefan was done he got to his feet. Three small incisions formed a triangle above the waistband of his boxers. Alex lifted up his shirt and showed his appendectomy scars to Stefan.

"Freaky," they both said at the same time.

"How long have you been playing?" Alex asked, gesturing to the guitar.

"Since I was five. My dad taught me."

"You must be good."

Stefan shrugged. Alex passed him the guitar. Stefan played a few chords of "Born in the U.S.A." "Better than the Boss," Alex said, only half-joking.

"Yeah, right." Stefan handed the guitar to Alex. Then he lay down on the floor and started doing his sit-ups.

Anna was in the kitchen, making pancake batter and

listening to some classical music on the radio. Alex watched her for a while from the doorway. She looked different, lighter, as if someone had removed the invisible weight that had always been on her shoulders. *It was no mystery*, he thought. For all those years she had thought that Stefan was dead. And now, as if by some miracle, he'd suddenly come back to life. *She should have told me about him*, Alex thought, but he wasn't angry about it anymore. All that mattered now was that he and Stefan were reunited. Everything else was ancient history.

"Morning, dude."

"Morning, Anna. Let's put blueberries in the batter," he suggested.

Boris and Stefan came into the kitchen a few minutes later. "I hope you guys like blueberry pancakes," Anna said.

"Stefan's favorite," Boris said.

"What time are we leaving?" Alex asked, as his mother took a third batch of pancakes out of the oven. Team Oregon had beaten Team Michigan the night before, knocking B.C. out of the medal round, and the four of them were going to Whistler for the weekend. In normal circumstances, Alex would have been disappointed at missing out on an opportunity to impress Bill Henry and the other college scouts, but these weren't what you would call normal circumstances. He had one week with his brother—one week to make up for seventeen years—and he wanted to spend every minute of it with him.

"I have to drop in at the store in Langley," his mom said, "but I won't be there long. I'd like to get out of here by one so we can beat the traffic. More pancakes, Boris?"

"No, thank you. They're delicious but I'm full."

Alex and Stefan held their plates up at the same time.

Anna divided the pancakes evenly between them.

Alex's cellphone beeped, alerting him to a text message. "Kenny says you can borrow his Brodie," he told Stefan after he read the message. "We'll bike to the peak of Whistler tomorrow. A mile of vertical." Mountain biking was another thing he and Stefan had in common.

"A mile of vertical?" Stefan asked, not understanding the term. Alex was about to explain when Boris hushed him. He leaned over and turned up the volume on the radio to listen to the news.

"… has won the election in Berovia, defeating the Freedom Party, which has governed the country for the past nineteen years. The new government is promising to co-operate with the International War Crimes Tribunal, which has indicted two Berovian generals, Milos Koralic and Anton Zarkov, for war crimes committed during the country's war with Maldania. During its time in power, the Freedom Party refused to arrest the two men, who are regarded as national heroes by many Berovians."

"Heroes," Boris snorted. "How can they call those butchers heroes after what they did at the Church of San Marco?"

"What did they do?" Alex asked.

"Those *heroes*," Boris said, spitting out the word, "forced two hundred and forty Maldans, including women and children, into the church, barred the doors, and then set it on fire."

"The Maldans were just as bad," Anna said.

"That's true," Boris responded, "but that doesn't mean they shouldn't pay for what they did."

Alex was thinking about all those people being burned alive when the doorbell rang.

"That will be Roman," Anna said. "Your uncle," she

said to Stefan. She turned to Boris. "We have a house rule here. No talk about the war."

"That's fine with me," Boris said.

Anna walked out of the kitchen. A few seconds later she came back with Roman.

"This is my brother, Roman Kuchar," Anna said, making the introductions as Boris and Stefan stood up. "This is Boris Divac." Roman and Boris exchanged a wary glance. "And this is his son, Stefan. Your nephew."

"Gardo je mi," they said to each other as they shook hands. *Nice to meet you.* "It's a miracle," Roman said, putting his hands on Stefan's shoulders and staring at him in disbelief. "It's a miracle," he said again, before he finally let go. Alex realized that his uncle had known about Stefan all along and that for all these years he, like Anna, had thought he was dead.

Anna poured Roman a cup of coffee. He looked at Alex and then back at Stefan. "They're like two peas in a pod. I hear you're a goalie, too," he said to Stefan.

"I am," Stefan said.

"He's amazing," Alex said. "You should have seen some of the saves he made against us."

"Maybe you'll both end up in the NHL," Roman said.

"For sure," Alex said. He looked at Stefan and rolled his eyes.

"You're going to love Whistler," Roman said. "The village is much newer, of course, but it reminds me of Varsoya." Varsoya was a town in Berovia. "Before it got destroyed by the bombing."

"A lot of towns in Maldania were destroyed by bombs, too," Boris said.

"Your army was shelling us from those towns," Roman answered.

"That's enough," Anna said forcefully.

"Your army did exactly the same thing," Boris said.

"Enough," Anna shouted in Berovian before Roman could reply. She glared at the two of them. "I don't want to hear another word about the war. That's all you people talk about. You're like little children. He started it. No, he started it," she said in a child's voice. "Not another word."

Boris and Roman squirmed in their chairs like two kids who'd just been scolded by their mother.

"Anna tells me you're in the travel business," Roman said politely after a few awkward seconds of silence.

"Yes. I have a small agency back home," Boris answered just as politely.

"There's a lot to see in Maldania," Roman said.

"We go to Berovia as well. One week in Maldania and one week in Berovia. The island is so small that we can go everywhere by bus. We try to have an equal number of Berovians and Maldans on the tour. I think it's important people understand that both sides suffered during the war. That's the only way we'll ever be able to move on."

"What a wonderful idea," Anna said.

"Interesting," Roman said, in a voice that made it clear he wasn't interested in the least. "How long have you had your agency?"

"About ten years. How about you?"

"Twenty-three. The business has changed since I got started. I used to be able to make a good living booking flights and hotels. But now, with the Internet, people do that for themselves. These days you've got to be a lot more creative. New sources of revenue. That's what my accountant calls it."

Alex and Stefan looked at each other. The conversation was about to get real boring. "You want to play some ball hockey?" Alex asked.

"That was heavy," Alex said to Stefan as they walked toward the garage.

"Heavy?"

"Intense. Emotional," Alex explained. He raised the garage door. "It must be terrible living somewhere where there's so much hatred."

"I don't hate anybody," Stefan said, "except guys who shoot the puck at my head."

"Did you know about San Marco?" Alex asked.

"Sure. It happened on January 27, the same day Dad got me at the orphanage. Every Maldan knows about it. Zarkov and Koralic, the two generals they talked about on the radio?" Alex nodded. "People say they were laughing when the church burned down."

"With all those people inside?" Alex asked.

Stefan nodded. "They're the two most hated men in Maldania."

"No wonder," Alex said. "Why did they do it?"

"There were a lot of Maldans living in Berovia when the war started. The Stork and the Snowman wanted to get rid of them. After they burned down San Marco, every Maldan in Berovia left the country."

"The Stork and the Snowman?"

"Zarkov is called the Stork because he's very tall and very thin. Koralic is the Snowman because he's got a round head on a round belly."

"The Stork and the Snowman," Alex said. "Sounds like a movie title."

The hockey net was on a shelf at the back of the garage. It was covered in cobwebs. Alex got up on a stepladder and passed the net down to Stefan. They carried it out of the garage and put it down in the driveway. Alex grabbed a pair of goalie pads, the ones he used when he was in Bantam, from a box of hockey equipment. "You want to go in goal first?" he asked.

"Sure," Stefan said. He strapped on the pads and grabbed the goalie stick and a baseball glove.

Alex took a tennis ball and a hockey stick and went to the end of the driveway. "Want to keep score?" he asked.

"No point if you don't."

"Switch after fifty shots?" Alex asked. Stefan nodded. Alex stickhandled toward the goal. Stefan got down in a crouch. Alex fired the ball low to the stick side. Stefan turned it aside easily.

Seventeen shots and seventeen saves later, Roman came out of the house. He went up to Stefan and hugged him tightly for a few seconds. "Have fun in Whistler. See you at the office when you get back," he said to Alex. He took a final look at Stefan, shook his head in amazement, and then got in his car and drove away.

Alex went upstairs on his next shot, a bullet that Stefan caught as casually as if they were playing catch. It took thirty-four shots before Alex finally squeezed one past his brother. It was the only goal he was able to score.

"You're too good," Alex said after he'd taken his fifty shots. They were about to switch positions when Anna and Boris came out of the house.

"Boris is coming to Langley with me," Anna said.

"Do I have time to show these boys a few tricks?" Boris asked. Anna nodded. Alex handed Boris his stick. He stickhandled toward Stefan, feinted to his glove side, and flicked a shot high to the stick side. Stefan blocked it with ease. "Not bad," Boris said. He took a few more shots—all of them hard and well placed—but none got past Stefan.

Anna cheered for every save.

"Time to retire, old man," Stefan said affectionately.

Boris handed the stick back to Alex. "Stefan used to drag me outside to practice no matter how bad the weather was," he recalled. "He would make me take shots at him for hours on end." Alex remembered that he used to drag Anna outside, too, but by the time he was ten there was no point. She couldn't shoot the ball hard enough to dent a piece of paper.

"Don't forget," Anna said. "We're leaving at one." She and Boris got in her car and drove off.

Alex put on the pads and took his place in front of the net. He saved the first eleven shots but Stefan scored on the twelfth, a slapshot from point-blank range that Alex got a piece of, but not enough to keep it from trickling into the net. Stefan only managed to score once more on Alex, but it was enough to give him a 2–1 win.

"Are you going to play for the same team as last year?" Alex asked after they put the net back in the garage.

"No," Stefan said. "I'm too old."

"So where are you going to play?"

"Nowhere."

"What do you mean?"

"There's nowhere to play once you turn eighteen. We don't have a junior league in Maldania. There are club teams but nobody takes it seriously."

"What about playing in another country in Europe? You're good enough to play anywhere."

"You can't just show up. You have to be scouted, and scouts don't come to Maldania. I was hoping something would happen here, but …" Stefan shrugged. Alex nodded. Team Maldania was so bad the scouts hadn't bothered showing up for their games.

"You mean you're finished playing hockey?" Alex asked. Stefan nodded. "That sucks," Alex said. "That really sucks."

"What?" Stefan asked. It was another expression he didn't know. But he figured it out soon enough from the context. "Yeah," he said. "That sucks. That really sucks."

"Is that Mom's report card?" Alex asked.

Stefan nodded. "From her last year of high school." He and Alex were in the living room waiting for Anna and Boris to get back from Langley so they could go to Whistler. They were looking through some of Anna's papers from Berovia that were in an envelope glued to the back cover of the photo album. Stefan was explaining them to Alex because they were written in Berovian, which had a different alphabet from English.

"What's this?" Alex asked, pointing to an official-looking document with a seal.

"Your father's death certificate."

"He's your father, too," Alex said.

"Only biologically. Boris is my real father. He's the one who raised me. He's the one who took care of me."

"Did you ever wonder who your biological parents were?" Alex asked.

"I did when Dad first told me I was adopted. But there was no way of finding out who they were so after a while I stopped thinking about it. I wasn't the only kid whose parents were killed in the war so I didn't feel like I was different. Lots of my friends were in the same situation."

"And now?"

"I don't know. It's weird. If Darko didn't die, I would have grown up with you guys. That would have been great"—*Yes, it would*, Alex thought—"but then I wouldn't have grown up with Dad and I can't imagine me without him." Alex nodded. He couldn't imagine himself without Anna, either. "This doesn't make sense," Stefan said a moment later, looking up from the death certificate.

"What doesn't?"

"It says here that Darko died on January 27."

"So?"

"That was the day he and I went to get the doctor, right?" Alex nodded. "But Dad—Boris—said he got me at the orphanage on the twenty-seventh. That's why he chose it as my birthday."

"Somebody must have found you and taken you to the orphanage after Dad—Darko—was killed," Alex said.

"The people at the orphanage said I'd already been there for a couple of days. How could I have been there before the twenty-seventh, before Darko died?"

"You couldn't … Didn't the Church of San Marco burn down on January 27?" Alex asked. He had a sinking feeling in the pit of his stomach.

"Yeah. Why? … Oh my God." Stefan stared at Alex. Alex nodded somberly. Anna had never told him how his father died. He had assumed that was because she didn't know. But she knew. She hadn't told him so he wouldn't know the truth—his father had been one of the victims of the massacre at San Marco.

Just then Anna and Boris came through the front door. "Are you guys ready to leave?" she asked. Then she saw the look on Alex's face.

"I was on the balcony of my apartment watering the plants when a man came running around the corner at full speed," Boris recalled. "He was carrying a small child. You and your father," he said to Stefan unnecessarily. "There was a hedge in front of the apartment building. Your father hid you behind the hedge and ran off.

"A few seconds later a truckload of Berovian soldiers turned the corner, coming from the same direction your father had. They had obviously been chasing him. When they caught up to him, the soldiers threw him into the back of the truck." Boris paused for a moment. "I waited until the truck drove off, and then I went outside and brought you back to the apartment."

He turned to Anna. "My wife and I thought Stefan might have family in Sarno but we couldn't ask any questions without putting us all in danger. We left for Maldania the next day."

"You had to leave. No Maldan was safe in Sarno after San Marco … You saved Stefan's life," Anna said, her voice cracking.

Boris shrugged. "Anybody would have done the same."

"If someone had seen you and turned you in, you would have been killed."

Boris shrugged again. "I couldn't just leave him there."

"Why didn't you tell me the truth?" Stefan asked.

"I thought about it," Boris said, "but I didn't know how it would affect you. And I was worried it would make you hate all Berovians. There are too many people like that."

He looked at Stefan, pleading for understanding. Anna gave Alex the same look.

Alex nodded to let her know it was okay. He knew his mother had wanted to spare him the pain of knowing how his father died. But now the secret was out in the open and it was out for good. He would just have to figure out a way to deal with the pain.

CHAPTER NINE

Alex lay in bed unable to sleep, plagued by the same thoughts that had kept him awake for the past three nights. No matter how hard he tried, he couldn't stop thinking about the horrifying way his father had died.

It seemed like hours before fatigue took over and he was finally able to fall asleep. When he woke up, he rolled onto his side and saw himself sleeping in another bed a few feet away. For a moment he thought he was dreaming.

Sunlight flooded through the bedroom window of the condo in Whistler. It had rained all weekend, but today he and Stefan would finally be able to bike to the peak.

Alex logged on to his computer and checked the International War Crimes Tribunal Twitter feed about the case against Zarkov and Koralic.

The two men had gone into hiding the day the new government came into power, and the authorities were determined to prevent them from leaving the island. Security at airports in both Berovia and Maldania had been doubled, and the government in Sarno had obtained the co-operation of all neighboring countries to ensure that every boat that left the island would be boarded and searched. With the escape routes cut off, the government was confident that it was only a matter of time until the two men were caught.

"Any news?" Stefan sat on the side of his bed, rubbing

the sleep out of his eyes. Alex shook his head. "They'll catch them eventually," Stefan predicted. "Everybody knows what they look like. They won't be able to stay in hiding forever." He stood up and went into the washroom.

Alex clicked on a photo of the two men standing beside each other. Stefan was right. These two couldn't exactly melt into a crowd.

Their nicknames had been well chosen. Milos "the Snowman" Koralic was bald, with a huge, round face atop an immense belly perched on a pair of fat legs. He was smoking a big cigar. If you looked quickly you could almost imagine it was a snowman's carrot nose. Anton "the Stork" Zarkov towered over him. He was as thin as the Snowman was fat. His narrow chest was supported by two spindly legs. His nose jutted out of his face like a beak. A jagged scar ran down the right side of his face.

The Stork held a gun in his huge left hand and he was laughing, apparently at something the Snowman had said. *Something funny*, Alex thought bitterly, *like burning a couple of hundred people alive.*

He was horrified by what they had done, but he wasn't surprised. He'd taken a course on genocide and crimes against humanity the previous year and he knew that human beings could do the most terrible things to each other. He'd learned about the Holocaust, where the Nazis killed millions of Jews in the gas chambers. He knew about the war in Rwanda, where 800,000 members of one tribe were butchered in only three months by the members of another tribe, many slaughtered by neighbors they had lived beside all their lives.

Those were only two examples. Crimes like those had happened over and over again throughout history. A couple of million deaths here, a few hundred thousand there. The numbers were so overwhelming that it was impossible to connect emotionally to what had happened. The true horror didn't hit him until the day a woman who had survived the slaughter in Rwanda came to talk to his class. When she told them how she had seen her entire family killed in front of her, when he could put a name and a face to the suffering, what had been an abstract historical event suddenly became very real.

It was the same with San Marco. It was not just an abstract historical event. Not when the name and the face belonged to his father.

"Hungry?" Boris asked when Alex came into the kitchen. "Stupid question. Teenage boys are always hungry. Do you like scrambled eggs?"

"Sure." Alex walked to the counter. Boris was chopping up some anchovies.

"They're for Stefan," Boris said. "I won't put them in your eggs."

"That's okay," Alex said. "I like anchovies." *The list keeps growing*, he thought. He poured himself a glass of juice, then sat down as Boris prepared breakfast. It was hard to imagine that this ordinary-looking man was a hero. But that's what he was. He had risked his life to save Stefan. Alex compared that to what the Stork and the Snowman had done. An image of them laughing as they watched the Church of San Marco go up in flames flashed in front of his eyes. It reminded him of something he'd read during his course. "People will do anything to, or for, each other." *That just about sums up the human race*, he thought.

"Good morning," Anna said, giving Alex a kiss on the cheek. A few seconds later Stefan came into the kitchen.

"Good morning, sweetie. How did you sleep?" Anna

asked gravely, as if a lot was riding on his answer.

"I slept good," Stefan said.

"I slept well," Anna corrected. She put her hand to Stefan's cheek, as if she needed to touch him to prove he was real.

"We'll meet you at the Brewhouse at one," Anna said. They were all standing by the gondola in Whistler Village.

"Okay," Alex answered. It was only nine thirty. That would give them plenty of time to ride up to the peak and back down again.

"Stay together so Stefan doesn't get lost," Anna instructed.

"You can't get lost," Alex said. "You just keep going up."

"Be careful," Anna said.

"Have fun," Boris said.

A group of Japanese tourists, all with cameras around their necks, walked by. One of the women did a double take when she saw Alex and Stefan. After three days of walking around Whistler with Stefan, Alex was used to the reaction. People were fascinated by twins. They thought nothing of approaching them with the stupidest questions. His personal favorite was the turkey who asked him if he felt pain when Stefan got hurt.

The woman motioned to her camera, silently asking for permission to take their picture. "What do you think?" Alex asked Stefan.

"It's okay with me." They put their arms around each other's shoulders and smiled for the camera.

"Say sushi," Alex said.

The woman politely nodded her thanks and took their picture. The rest of the group immediately pulled out their cameras and snapped away. Then they all bowed and walked off.

"Let's go," Alex said. He led the way to the start of the bike path. "There's the peak," he said, pointing straight up.

"A mile of vertical," Stefan said. He was a quick study.

Two hours later Alex sprinted up the last hill and coasted to a stop at the peak. A few seconds later Stefan rode up beside him.

"That was great," he said, clapping Alex on the back. Anna's fear that Stefan would be left behind was groundless. He had stayed on Alex's rear tire the entire way up, even when Alex had put it in top gear. Alex couldn't have pulled away from him even if he'd wanted to.

The boys leaned their bikes against a tree. They stared at the mountains that spread out in front of them in all directions as far as they could see. Even though it was late August, snow still capped the distant peaks.

"It's beautiful," Stefan said in an awed voice.

"It is," Alex agreed. He'd been up here countless times over the years, but today, with his brother standing by his side, it felt like he was seeing it for the first time.

Stefan took a camera out of his knapsack. He backed up a few paces, put the camera on a rock, and looked through the viewfinder. "Move a step to the left," he said. Alex moved. Stefan pushed a button on the camera and sauntered over to Alex. He put his arm around his shoulders. "Say sushi," he said.

Alex and Stefan got to the Brewhouse a couple of minutes before one o'clock. They locked up their bikes and walked into the restaurant. Boris and Anna were sitting opposite each other at a table by the window.

"How was the ride?" Anna asked Stefan. She patted the

seat beside her.

"Fantastic." Stefan slid into the chair. Alex sat down beside Boris. Anna reached over and brushed a lock of hair off Stefan's forehead. *She is really going to miss him when he goes back to Maldania*, Alex thought. *And so will I.* The waitress, young and cute, came over to their table. Her nametag identified her as Kyla from Adelaide, Australia. There were always a lot of Aussies working at Whistler.

She looked at Alex, then at Stefan, then back at Alex.

"That's why we dress them differently," Anna joked. Stefan was wearing a red biking shirt. Alex wore a blue one.

Kyla laughed. "What can I get you?" she asked.

"I'll have the Greek salad," Anna said. "And a coffee."

"The chicken sandwich, please," said Boris. "And another Kokanee," he added, pointing to his beer.

Kyla looked at Stefan. "The burgers are great here," Alex suggested.

"Sounds good. I'll have a burger," Stefan said.

"Anything to drink?" Kyla asked.

"I'll have one of those," Stefan said, pointing to Boris's beer.

"No you won't," Anna and Boris said at the same time.

"Chocolate milkshake," Stefan said.

"I'll have the burger, too," Alex said. "And a vanilla milkshake."

"Excellent," Kyla said, slipping her order pad into a pocket of her uniform.

"For the first few months we actually did dress you in different colors," Anna said after Kyla walked away. "It was the only way we could tell you apart, except for the mole Stefan has at the base of his spine." Boris nodded. He was familiar with the mole. "It was either dress you differently or pull your pants down every time we wanted to know who was who," she joked. "After a few months we didn't need to do it anymore. The differences between you started to come out."

"Like what?" Stefan asked.

"Facial gestures. The way you moved. Things only a parent would notice."

"You and Alex could be wearing masks and I'd still know which one was you," Boris said to Stefan.

"Your personalities were different, too," Anna went on. "Alex was more cautious than Stefan. Stefan would always be the first to try something new. Once he did it, Alex would do it too."

"That's what a big brother is for," Stefan joked.

"You two should go wash up," Anna said.

"I left my computer on my bike," Alex said to Stefan as they left the table. "The washroom's there." He pointed and went outside.

When he returned, Kyla was clearing off a table near the entrance. "Hey," she said with a friendly smile. Alex frantically tried to think of something to say, but all he could come up with was "Hey." He gave her a weak smile and headed to the washroom. *You've got all the moves*, the Voice said.

Stefan was drying his hands with a paper towel. Alex went to the sink and washed his hands. "Let's change shirts," Stefan said. "See if they notice." They swapped shirts and walked out of the washroom.

Kyla smiled at Alex again. "Hope you can make it tonight," she said. "Bring your brother."

"Uh, okay," Alex said in a puzzled voice. Kyla looked at him as if he was slightly deranged. "What was that all about?" Alex asked Stefan as they walked toward the table. "Make it where?"

"Kyla and her roommates are having a party," Stefan said nonchalantly. "We've been invited."

It took Alex a moment to put it together. Kyla thought he was Stefan because he was wearing the blue shirt. In the two minutes Alex had been outside collecting his bike computer, his brother had managed to get a beautiful girl to invite him to a party. And all he'd been able to do was say "Hey."

Stefan, wearing Alex's red shirt, sat down in the chair beside his father. Alex sat down beside his mother.

"Hungry?" his mother asked. Alex just nodded, knowing his voice would give the game away. "How about you?" she asked Stefan. He nodded too.

Boris's cellphone rang. He flipped it open. "Hello ... Roman," he said in a surprised voice. "How are you? ... It can't hurt to talk ... We're leaving here first thing in the morning ... I'll see you at one o'clock ... *Vo dinya.*" He hung up and turned to the others. "Roman wants to talk about going into business together. He thinks some of his clients would be interested in doing the tour of Maldania and Berovia."

"He didn't seem very interested when you mentioned it at the house," Anna said.

"Apparently his marketing manager, Tomas ..." Boris couldn't come up with his last name.

"Tomas Radich," Anna said.

Boris nodded. "Tomas convinced him it was a good idea. He thinks the press will eat it up. Berovians and Maldans working together for peace."

What a load of crap, Alex thought. *All Tomas cares about is earning a big fat commission so he can send Lina to private school and get Maria off his case.*

"Wonders will never cease," Anna said. "Roman going

into business with a Maldan. He must be mellowing. Or desperate."

"At this point we're just going to talk," Boris said. "Who knows if anything is going to happen."

Kyla arrived with their drinks. She gave Boris his beer, Anna her coffee, and, thinking Alex was Stefan, gave him the chocolate milkshake and Stefan the vanilla. After Kyla walked away, Stefan and Alex traded shakes.

"Very funny," Anna said, as she realized what had happened.

"What's going on?" Boris asked.

"You two could be wearing masks and I'd still know which one was you," Stefan said, repeating his father's words. Alex and Anna laughed.

"I knew it was you," Boris said. Everyone laughed again. "What?" he protested. "You think I don't know my own son? I was just waiting to see how long it would take Anna to figure it out."

"These two were so cute when they were little," Anna said to Boris. Alex and Stefan both made a gagging motion. "You should have seen them in their crib. They slept holding on to each other. I remember once," she said, chuckling at the memory, "Stefan had a cold and the doctor said he should sleep by himself so Alex wouldn't get sick. They both cried bloody murder for hours until we gave in and put them back together. The next day Alex came down with a cold. It was a bad one, but anything was better than listening to the two of them cry. They couldn't stand to be separated from each other."

Alex looked at Stefan. He knew his brother was thinking the same thing he was. They couldn't stand to be separated, and yet the day after tomorrow that was exactly what was going to happen.

CHAPTER TEN

Alex sat on a chair in Stefan's room, watching his brother finish packing. Neither of them had uttered more than a couple of words in the past hour. There was nothing to say. Alex looked at his watch for the umpteenth time. Fifteen minutes until they had to leave for the airport.

It was hard to believe it had only been seven days since he and Stefan had stood at center ice, staring at each other in disbelief. Seven days that had passed in a blur, but had changed his life forever. The feeling he had carried with him as far back as he could remember, the feeling that a part of him was missing, was gone. Gone for good.

Alex looked at his watch again. Twelve minutes. He tried to console himself with the thought that Stefan was coming back for the Christmas holidays, but that was more than five months from now.

Stefan zipped his suitcase shut. "I got this for you," he said, handing Alex a gift-wrapped package about the size of a book.

"I have something for you, too," Alex said. He had bought Stefan Pro Hockey 13, the latest version of the video game. It cost more than he wanted to spend, but what the heck, he only had one brother. "You first," Alex said.

Stefan unwrapped his present. As soon as he saw what it was, he started laughing. Alex was about to ask Stefan what was up when he realized why he was laughing. "You're kidding?" he said. Stefan shook his head. Alex started laughing, too. By the time he unwrapped his copy of Pro Hockey 13, both boys were laughing so hard that tears were streaming down their faces.

Just as they were starting to settle down, Anna popped her head into the office. "What's with you two?" she asked, setting them off again. "We have to leave in five minutes," she added. That sobered them up in a hurry.

"We'll be right down," Alex said. His mom nodded and walked away.

"This sucks," Stefan said. "This really sucks."

"I'm going to miss you, man," Alex said.

"Me, too."

"Christmas will be here before we know it," Alex said.

"For sure." Stefan grabbed his suitcase. As they headed for the door, the phone on their mom's desk rang. Alex picked it up.

"Hello."

"Is this Alex?" The voice was familiar, but Alex couldn't place it.

"Yes."

"It's Coach McAndrew."

"Coach," Alex said, surprised.

"I want to get in touch with your brother. Do you have his email address? Or a phone number where I can reach him?"

"He's right here," Alex said. He passed the phone to Stefan. "It's Coach McAndrew," he whispered. "From Team B.C."

Stefan took the phone. "Hello … Thank you … Are you serious? … Of course I'd be interested." A stunned look crossed his face. "My father is here. I'll go get him."

59

Stefan put the phone down and looked at Alex.

"What is it?" Alex asked.

"He wants me to play for his team in West Vancouver."

"That's unbelievable. Unfreakingbelievable."

"Yeah," Stefan said. "Unfreakingbelievable."

The mood at the airport was the complete opposite of what Alex had imagined only an hour earlier. Joy instead of gloom. Excited chatter instead of subdued conversation. Anticipation instead of regret.

The only downer was that Stefan couldn't stay in Vancouver while all the details were being sorted out. He would need a student visa but the rule was that you had to apply from outside the country. Anna had called her Member of Parliament, who said he would do everything he could to fast-track Stefan's application, but he couldn't say how long it was going to take.

"It was a pleasure meeting you, Anna," Boris said when it was time for him and Stefan to go through security. They said goodbye Berovian style, with a kiss on one cheek, then the other, and then the first one again.

"I'll see you soon, I hope," Anna said.

How soon depended on when Stefan's visa came through. Boris and Roman had decided to go into business together after all, and had organized a tour of Berovia and Maldania beginning in mid-August. If Stefan got his visa before the tour started, Boris would return with him to Vancouver to help him get settled in and then would leave for Maldania with the tour. If that didn't work out, Boris would come for a visit sometime during the fall.

"Take care of yourself, Alex," Boris said.

"You, too."

Anna and Stefan hugged goodbye. Anna had tears in her eyes, as if she were afraid of losing him again.

"Later, bro," Stefan said to Alex after Anna finally let him go. They gave each other the athlete's hug, their forearms between their bodies as they leaned in to each other. "Skype me when you get home, dude," Alex said. They jabbed fists, and then Stefan and Boris grabbed their suitcases and wheeled them toward security.

"I feel sorry for Boris," Anna said after they disappeared. "This must be very hard on him."

"I guess," Alex said, although the thought hadn't occurred to him. He'd been too wrapped up in the excitement to think about anything other than Stefan's return, but it didn't take a lot of imagination to realize how Boris felt. As happy as he was to see Stefan reunited with his mother and brother, and for him to be able to continue his hockey career, Boris had to be sad that he would be so far away from his son. But he didn't hesitate when Stefan asked if he could move to Vancouver. Alex knew his mother would have done the same if the situation were reversed.

He put his arm around his mother's shoulders and leaned down to give her a kiss.

"What's that for?" she asked.

"Do I need a reason?"

Alex found himself thinking about the upcoming hockey season as he drove down Granville on the way home from the airport. In all the years he'd played hockey, he'd never been on a championship team. This year his Richmond team had a legitimate chance. Everybody was back from the squad that almost upset West Vancouver, the eventual league champs, in the playoffs the previous year, and West

Van had lost a number of its best players, including their starting goaltender. *Correction*, Alex said to himself. *That hole has just been filled.*

Alex had more than the championship at stake. If he continued to play the way he had been, he just might get that scholarship to the University of Minnesota. *You got some serious game.* He got chills just thinking about the compliment Bill Henry gave him. *Don't count your chickens before they hatch*, the Voice warned. *He hasn't seen your brother play.*

"I still can't believe this has happened," Anna said, interrupting Alex's thoughts. "It's like a fairy tale. I have to keep pinching myself to prove I'm not dreaming."

Alex nodded. It *was* like a fairy tale. So why did he have the feeling that everybody wasn't going to live happily ever after?

CHAPTER ELEVEN

Alex was barely winded by the time he finished his five mile run. The workout program he'd started a month earlier, the day after Stefan and Boris returned to Maldania, was paying dividends. Hockey practice started in two weeks, the same day school started, and he was determined to be in the best shape of his life by then.

In addition to his daily run, he was lifting weights five times a week, following the same program Lou Roberts used. Some people thought goalies didn't have to be in great shape because they stayed in the net all game, but that just wasn't true. A goalie needed strength and balance to move quickly, and the stamina to last an entire game. It was no coincidence that Lou Roberts could do more chin-ups than anybody else on the Canucks.

After he showered, Alex logged on to his computer and fired off an email to Stefan. *Any news?* The Canadian embassy in Sarno had said his visa would arrive any day. Stefan got back to him right away. *Still waiting.*

There was no progress in the hunt for the Stork and the Snowman either. A couple of weeks earlier the Berovian government had put up a hundred-thousand-dollar reward for information leading to the arrest of either man. The authorities believed the two men were holed up in one of the many remote mountain villages that dotted the country's rugged landscape. They would need help to survive and the government hoped the reward would persuade one of their supporters to turn them in.

So far there had been no takers and today was no different. Alex felt discouraged. Everyone believed the two men would try to escape from Berovia and find refuge elsewhere, where they weren't so well known, and each day that went by without their capture increased their chances of getting away.

Alex arrived at the agency at ten o'clock. A note from Tomas was taped to his computer. *Bring me the revised itinerary as soon as you get in.* The tour to Berovia and Maldania had started a couple of days earlier and the itinerary was constantly changing.

Alex took the latest version of the itinerary into Tomas's office. Tomas wasn't there so Alex put it on his desk. He noticed that a website for a plastic surgeon was on Tomas's computer screen, with "before" and "after" pictures of patients who'd undergone various procedures.

"Maria thinks Lina needs to have her nose straightened," Tomas said as he entered his office.

"I never noticed anything wrong with her nose."

"That's what I keep telling Maria. You know how much something like that costs?" He didn't wait for Alex to answer. "Five thousand dollars." He shook his head in disgust. "Is that the itinerary?" Alex handed it to him. Tomas read it over. "Perfect. Email it to Boris right away."

Alex had just sent it off when Lara came out of Roman's office. She grabbed her purse.

"See you later," she said.

"Where are you going?"

"Passport office. Roman wants me to pick up Sophia's passport." Sophia was Roman's wife.

"I guess you're done for the day," Alex joked.

"You know what those lineups are like."

A few minutes after Lara left the front door swung open and Peter Jurak entered the office. Peter was Greta's boyfriend as well as a friend of Roman and Tomas, and another member of the Berovian Mafia.

"Hey," he said to Alex, whose desk was closest to the door. He held out his fist. Alex bumped it. Peter was the only adult Alex knew who could fist-bump without looking like a dork.

"That was fun the other day," Alex said.

"Glad you enjoyed it." Peter was a makeup artist for the movies, and the week before he'd invited Alex and Lara to the set of a martial arts movie starring their favorite actor, Johnny Chin. When they arrived, Peter came out of a trailer with an old man whose face had more lines than a road map. It was only when he said hello that they realized it was Johnny Chin.

"Are you working on another movie?" Alex asked.

"Leaving today for a gig in Hungary," Peter said. "*Vampire Killers 3*." He held his nose to indicate that it was a real stinker. "I don't want to go but if I was choosy about the movies I worked on, I'd be eating at the food bank."

Peter caught Greta's eye and gave her a big smile. The two of them had been going out for over a year. At first Greta wouldn't give him the time of day, but even though Peter didn't suffer from a lack of women—"He's a make-*out* artist, not a make*up* artist," Roman liked to say—he wouldn't take no for an answer. "Why keep hitting your head against the wall?" Roman asked him once. Alex still remembered Peter's response: "You can't win the lottery if you don't buy a ticket." And going out with Greta was definitely like winning the lottery.

Greta came up to them. "I'm taking Peter to the airport," she said to Alex. "I'll be back in an hour or so." She and Peter walked out of the agency hand-in-hand.

Lara still hadn't returned by mid-morning when Roman sent Alex out on an espresso run. This time he was definitely going to ask Jenna out. *No more wimping out*, he said to himself, psyching himself up as he pulled open the door to the café. *You can't win the lottery if you don't buy a ticket.*

Jenna was working the cash. She smiled at Alex as he walked to the counter. *The worst that can happen is that she says no*, he told himself.

"Hey, Alex," Jenna said. "How are you doing?"

"I'm good." Alex could feel his resolve vanish into thin air. "Two espressos, please," he said.

Jenna called out the order to the barista and rang up the sale. Alex paid her and stepped to the side. He felt about two feet tall.

He was still beating himself up about it when he got back to the agency. Roman was on the phone. Tomas was sitting on the couch.

"It's past seven o'clock in Italy. You'll have to wait until the morning to call the doctor. Okay, see you for dinner," Roman said into the phone.

"How's Sophia's grandfather?" Tomas asked.

"Not good. Not good at all." Roman turned to Alex. "Boris called," he said. "Stefan finally got his visa. He's coming back with the tour on the thirty-first. Isn't that fantastic?"

"Fantastic," Alex said, but he had to force himself to sound enthusiastic. His brother would be here in ten days. He'd been waiting for this moment ever since he and Anna took Stefan to the airport. Heck, he'd been waiting for it his whole life. So why didn't he feel more excited about it?

CHAPTER TWELVE

By the time the big day arrived, Alex understood why he was so ambivalent about his brother's arrival. It all came down to hockey. This was supposed to be his year. He had it all mapped out. First team all-star, maybe even the league MVP for him, and a league championship for the Richmond Cougars. Stefan's appearance on the scene threatened to upset the apple cart.

Alex stepped off the bus across from the travel agency just as Lara got out of her mother's red Honda Element.

"You must be excited," she said. "I can't wait to meet Stefan."

"He's looking forward to meeting you, too."

"I can't believe summer's over already," Lara said.

"I can't believe school starts on Tuesday."

"I know. What a drag."

They forgot all about school as soon as they stepped into the agency. Everybody was in a frenzy. The tour's return flight to Vancouver from Berovia had been delayed because of a bomb threat at the airport in Sarno. Boris had taken everyone to a nearby hotel so there was no danger, but nobody knew when the flight would be able to take off. Lara and Alex were kept busy all morning answering calls from anxious relatives.

"Where's the Jameson file?" Tomas barked, as he flipped through the top drawer of the filing cabinet. He'd been in a foul mood all day.

"It should be there," Lara said.

"Well, it's not," Tomas snapped.

It took Lara all of ten seconds to find the file. She handed it to him. "You're welcome," she said sarcastically when he didn't thank her.

Just before noon Roman came out of his office. "Boris called," he announced. "They're on their way to the airport. The flight leaves in an hour. It's due in around ten."

Everybody clapped. "Start calling people back and let them know what's happening," Roman said to Alex and Lara. He came up beside Tomas. "Boris said he saw Peter in Sarno yesterday, getting into a taxi with a tall blonde," he whispered, glancing at Greta to make sure she couldn't hear. "I thought he was working on a movie in Hungary."

"So did I," Tomas said.

"I can't believe Peter's such a sleaze bucket," Lara said to Alex after Tomas and Roman returned to their offices.

"Maybe there's an innocent explanation," Alex suggested, although he couldn't think of one.

"Yeah, right," Lara said.

"Peter's crazy about Greta. It doesn't make any sense."

"Sense has nothing to do with it. When it comes to sex, men don't think with their heads," Lara said, emphasizing the word *head* to make it clear she thought another part of the male anatomy was making the decisions.

I don't believe it, Alex said to himself. Peter wouldn't go all the way to Berovia just to have sex. He wasn't that desperate. *Unlike me*, he thought. He'd walk from Hungary to Berovia if it meant he was finally going to get laid. Walk! Hell, he'd crawl.

The family members waiting for the tour group stood in

front of the arrival doors at Vancouver International Airport. They were huddled into two separate groups. Alex knew that one group was Maldan and the other Berovian, although you couldn't tell them apart by looking at them.

"He's here," Anna said excitedly as the flight status for Air Berovia Flight 517 from Sarno changed to "landed" on the arrivals monitor.

It was another twenty minutes before the first tour group member came through the arrivals door, identifiable by the bright orange tag with the name of Roman's agency attached to his suitcase.

Roman handed Alex a stack of restaurant vouchers for their clients. It was a goodwill gesture to compensate them for the delay, even though it hadn't been the agency's fault. "You take that side," he said, pointing to the left side of the ramp leading out from the arrivals door. "I'll take this one."

A fat man with long black hair and a goatee was the first to come down Alex's side of the ramp. "Did you enjoy the tour?" Alex asked as he handed the man a voucher. The man nodded. Alex noticed that he had one brown eye and one green eye, just like Lou Roberts.

The arriving passengers received emotional welcomes from their family members. Even though there had been no real danger from the bomb threat, the relief on everybody's faces was visible. The two groups gradually mingled into one as the Maldans and Berovians who'd been on the tour said goodbye to one another.

Stefan was among the last group to arrive, pulling a huge suitcase and carrying his guitar. The moment Alex saw his brother all his misgivings vanished. He watched happily as Anna wrapped her arms around Stefan. The two boys beamed at each other. They were back together, and this time it was for good.

CHAPTER THIRTEEN

"Good luck, sweetie," Anna said to Stefan as she pulled up in front of the school. "I'm sure everything will be fine," she added in a reassuring voice. "You'll have some new friends before you know it."

Stefan smiled. If he was nervous for his first day of school in a new country, he sure didn't show it.

"Mr. Dowd," Anna said, referring to the school principal, "told me all your teachers are expecting you, and that they'll do whatever they can to make sure you don't have any trouble keeping up."

"Great," Stefan said with a smile. He didn't seem too worried about that either.

"If nobody comes to pick you up for your practice, call me and I'll come get you," Anna said to Stefan, popping the trunk so he and Alex could get their hockey bags. They both had practice after school. Coach McAndrew had arranged for Stefan to get a ride to West Van.

"I will," Stefan said patiently. They'd been through this a million times.

"Did you remember to pack an apple for his teacher?" Alex asked Anna.

"Very funny," she said.

"An apple?" Stefan asked after Anna drove away. "You Canadians are weird," he said after Alex explained the saying. "In Maldania we give our teacher a bottle of slivovitz." Slivovitz was a kind of plum brandy that was popular in Berovia and Maldania. It was Roman's favorite drink.

"You're kidding!" Alex said before he realized that Stefan was joking.

Freddie Curry and Kenny Nelson were standing by the front door.

"Holy shit," Freddie said. "I knew I had too much to drink last night."

"Say hello to Kenny Nelson," Alex said to Stefan, pointing at Kenny. "You can ignore the other guy. Everybody else does. This is my brother, Stefan."

"Nice to meet you, Stefan," Kenny said. "Welcome to Canada."

"I'm Fred Curry," Fred said. He gestured to the school. "Welcome to hell."

"Kenny plays for Richmond," Alex told Stefan. "He was on Team B.C. He scored the first goal against your team."

"Left wing. Number 11," Stefan said by way of identification, to the amazement of both Kenny and Alex. "Wrist shot from the face-off circle. Nice shot."

"You were screened," Kenny said. "West Van's chances of repeating just got a lot better," he said to Alex.

"That's for sure. We'd better get going," Alex said to Stefan. "Dowd's waiting for you."

Alex sat in math class staring out the window, waiting for school to end. He was eager to get to hockey practice. It was the first practice of the season and he'd been thinking about it all day.

A pigeon landed on the steeple of the church across the street, reminding Alex of San Marco. Nearly two months had passed since the Stork and the Snowman went into hiding and Alex wondered if they had managed to escape from Berovia. The government claimed it was checking every vessel that left the island, but the Italian coast was less than a hundred miles away, only three hours by motorboat, and if the trip was made at night a boat could easily avoid detection, no matter what the authorities said."

The bell went off, interrupting Alex's thoughts and triggering a mass exodus from the classroom. Alex saw Stefan standing by his locker talking to Emma Robinson. She was laughing at something he said. *You've got to be kidding*, Alex said to himself. *Emma Robinson? On his first day?* Emma was one of the hottest girls in the school. Emma laughed again, putting her hand on Stefan's arm for a second, and walked away.

"Hey," Alex said as he joined Stefan. "Mom will be glad to hear you made a new friend." He nodded toward Emma. Stefan shrugged. All in a day's work. "How did it go?" Alex asked.

"Pretty good," Stefan said. "Although everybody kept calling me Alex. The teachers seem nice. Except for chemistry."

"Who do you have?"

"Mr. Garnett."

"I had him last year. He sucks. Too bad you're not in my class. Mr. Pearce is great."

They walked to the phys ed office to collect their hockey bags and went out the front entrance. Lara was standing on the steps. She rubbed her eyes in an exaggerated motion when she saw the two of them, as if she was seeing double.

Alex gave her a wry smile. "Now say something original, like 'How do people tell you two apart?'"

"It's easy to tell you apart," Lara said. "He's the good-looking one."

"That's what I keep telling him," Stefan said.

"I'm Lara," she said. "It's great to finally meet you. Alex has told me a lot about you."

"Stefan." They shook hands.

Before they could say anything else, a car horn blared. Lara's boyfriend, Jason, was parked in front of the school in a neon-green Ford Mustang GT.

"Nice ride," Alex said. "The color looks like puke."

"Jealousy is one of the seven deadly sins," Lara said. "Nice meeting you, Stefan. I'll see you guys later." She hurried down the path and got into Jason's car. *I'm not jealous*, Alex thought. *I just can't believe you're with that jerk.*

"She's cute," Stefan said as Jason pulled away.

"I guess."

"Did you and Lara go out together?"

"No, man. Why?"

"I don't know. Just seemed like it."

"I don't like her boyfriend. That's all. I don't think about Lara like that. We've known each other since we were little kids."

"She's not a little kid anymore."

That seems to be the consensus, Alex said to himself.

A Toyota Corolla pulled up across the street. Paul Collins, one of the West Van players, got out of the car.

"Here's your lift," Alex said. He and Stefan walked down the steps, drawing stares from the students who were milling around the school entrance. "We should start dressing the same," Alex said. "That would really give them something to stare at."

Paul looked at the two of them as they approached, clearly trying to figure out who was who.

"Hey, Paul," Alex said, making it easy for him.

"Hey, Alex. I'm Paul," he said to Stefan.

"Stefan."

"Toss your bag in the trunk," Paul said. He pushed a button on his car key, popping the trunk open. Stefan put his bag into the trunk and walked to the passenger door.

"Everybody's saying you guys are the team to beat this year," Paul said to Alex.

"Shouldn't you wait until later in the season before you start messing with my head?"

Paul laughed. "All I'm saying is that we lost some of our best players. Nick, Ivan, Biggie, Red. You guys got everybody back."

Alex thought about what Paul said as they drove off. He knew it was way too early to start thinking about the championship, but maybe Paul was right. Maybe this would be the year. *For the team. And for me.*

The Richmond locker room was buzzing before practice. There was the typical start-of-the-season excitement in the room, but also a sense of purpose. Everybody felt the way Alex did. This could be their year. Anything less than the championship just wasn't going to cut it.

Earl Bales sat across the room, putting on his equipment. He was the backup goalie, one of two new players on the team. He was a big kid, bigger than Alex even though he was two years younger. He was talented, too. Alex had seen Bales play during the tryouts and he knew he wasn't going to have any trouble stepping up to Midget from Bantam.

Bales caught Alex's eye and held his gaze for a moment. *I know you've got the starting position all locked up*, his look seemed to say, *but I'll be ready if you screw up.* Alex remembered his first year on the team, when he was the new kid. He'd been happy to take a backup role and wait his turn. Bales was made from a different mold.

Neil Daniels, the team manager, walked around the room from player to player, giving out practice jerseys.

Neil handed a jersey to Alex. "I saw you play against Team Oregon," he said. "You were great."

"Thanks, Pie," Alex said, addressing Neil by his nickname.

"Hey, Pie," Mike Leonard shouted. Leonard was the one who hung the nickname on Neil. It had started out as Pizza Pie because Neil's face was covered with pimples, but after a couple of months it was shortened to Pie. "This is a medium. I need a large." He threw the jersey on the floor.

"Sorry, Mike," Neil said. He gave him a large and picked the medium off the floor.

"Sorry, Mike," Leonard repeated in a mocking voice. "Faggot," he said, uttering the word in a pretend cough. Half the team laughed. The other half looked down at their skates.

"Play nice, Mike," said Stevie Ryan, Leonard's best friend on the team. "Pie's got a crush on you. Isn't that right, Pie?"

Neil ignored him.

"He is kind of cute," Mike said. Then he coughed the word *faggot* again.

He's such a dick, Alex thought. He felt like saying something but there was no point. And anyway, Neil didn't seem to mind.

The room went silent when Coach Jed Hampton entered. He had a serious expression on his face. "A lot of you guys are throwing around the word 'championship,'" he said. "I've heard the talk. 'It's our year.' 'We've got

everybody back and look how close we came last year.'
'The teams that finished ahead of us lost their best
players.'" He looked around the room, making eye contact
with each player. "Talk is cheap, boys. Championships
aren't won in the locker room in September. They're won
on the ice in March. Between now and then every one of
you has to give 100 percent, 100 percent of the time. We're
on a seven-month journey, gentlemen. Today is just day
one." Hampton pivoted and walked out of the room
without another word.

"You heard Coach," Kenny Nelson, the team captain,
yelled. "Day one. Day one." The rest of the team took up
the chant as they took to the ice. "Day one. Day one."

Alex got home from practice a little before eight. The
house was empty. His mom was still at work and Stefan
hadn't yet returned from his practice. Alex turned on the
TV to watch *SportsCenter*. The big news was that the
Canucks had signed a six-foot-eight defenseman from
Slovakia with a reputation as a real bruiser. Lou Roberts
would be pleased about that, Alex thought. Every goalie
wanted a big defenseman who could clear the opponents
out from in front of the net.

He was mindlessly channel surfing after the sports
ended when a news item on CNN caught his attention.
"Koralic Escapes" was written across the screen. Alex
turned up the volume.

"For some analysis we have Ellen Baker, a senior
fellow at the Crocker Institute in Washington," the CNN
anchor, a middle-aged man with a white beard, said.
"Thanks for joining us, Ellen. What's your take on the
situation?"

The camera cut to Ellen Baker, a young woman with

long brown hair. "We can be fairly certain of two things," she said. "First, in all likelihood the general made his escape by boat. It's virtually inconceivable that he would be able to get on a plane given the added security measures that are in place. Second, he would probably have headed for the nearest landfall, near the town of Bari on the coast of Italy." A map came up on screen illustrating her point.

Alex felt the air go out of him. *So much for cutting off all the escape routes.*

"How likely is it that he'll be able to stay in hiding there?" the CNN anchor asked.

"I don't think he plans to stay," Baker answered. "The Italians have always sided with the Maldans against the Berovians, so he won't have many supporters there. My feeling is that he'll go to a country with a significant Berovian community where he can get the help he needs. That narrows it down to a handful of countries in Western Europe as well as the United States and Canada."

Canada, Alex repeated to himself.

"What are the chances of capturing him?"

"If it's going to happen, it will have to happen soon. The concern, of course, is that General Koralic will undergo plastic surgery to disguise his appearance, as others have done before him. If that happens, all bets are off."

"Thank you, Ms. Baker. We'll be keeping an eye on this story. Meanwhile, a Beverly Hills teenager has sued her mother for posting an unflattering picture of her on Facebook. The girl's lawyer ..."

Alex turned off the TV. If he was discouraged before, he was despairing now. If the Snowman had plastic surgery, nobody would ever find him.

It wasn't until Alex was in bed and about to drift off to

sleep that he remembered he'd seen a website for a plastic surgeon on Tomas's computer a few weeks earlier. The memory jolted him into consciousness. Tomas had said Maria wanted Lina to get her nose straightened, he recalled, but he might just have said that for Alex's benefit. One thing for sure, Lina didn't need a nose job. *Was it possible Tomas was involved in the Snowman's escape?* he wondered. *No way*, he decided a few seconds later. That kind of coincidence only happens in the movies.

CHAPTER FOURTEEN

In the three weeks following Koralic's escape, the Internet was full of rumors of his whereabouts. There was no reason to give the one that he was in Canada any more credibility than the ones that placed him in a dozen other countries around the world, but every time Alex heard it, he couldn't help thinking about the website for the plastic surgeon that he'd seen on Tomas's computer. And every time he did he came to the same conclusion he'd come to the first time. No way Tomas was involved. Things like that just didn't happen in real life. The bottom line was that nobody had a clue where the Snowman was. For all anybody knew he could still be in Italy, if in fact he'd gone there in the first place, and there was no proof of that either.

It was a slow morning at the travel agency and Alex was looking at a list of second-hand Vespas he'd printed off the Internet. He could get a decent one for around $3500. He'd saved $2500 during the summer, which meant he only needed another thousand. As long as he kept his marks up, Anna had agreed he could work one day every weekend at the travel agency during the school year. If he was careful, he'd have enough saved up by March break to buy the scooter. The timing was perfect, he thought. Just when the weather would be getting nice.

His mom called a little after ten. "The reporter for the

Sun called. The interview's been pushed back to Wednesday afternoon. She's going to meet you and Stefan at the school at four."

"Okay," Alex said. "That's the price of fame," he jokingly complained to Lara after he and his mom said goodbye. "Everybody wants a piece of you."

"I think I'll call the reporter," Lara said. "Give her the real story."

"What's it going to cost me to stop you from doing that?" Alex asked.

Tomas came out of his office before Lara could answer. "Can one of you stay on until six tonight?" he asked. "Roman and I have to leave at four thirty for a meeting and the printer said he might not be able deliver the brochures for the Greek Island cruise until the end of the day. We need them for the presentation on Monday."

"I can't," Lara said. "I have practice at four."

"I can stay," Alex said, happy to have the extra hours. Every little bit helped.

Peter Jurak arrived just before one.

"How was the shoot in Hungary?" Alex asked.

"Worst movie ever but they paid in cash. Afternoon, Lara," Peter said.

Lara grunted without looking up from her computer. Peter looked at Alex. *What's with her?* Alex shrugged but by then Peter's attention had moved on to Greta, who was hurrying toward him.

Lara stared at Peter's back. "Shithead," she muttered in a low voice. If looks could kill he'd be a dead man.

Greta and Peter hugged. "I really missed you," he said.

"I missed you, too," Greta said. "How was the flight?"

"Bumpy. We had to keep our seatbelts on the whole time."

"Welcome home," Tomas said, as he stepped out of his office.

"Thanks. I brought you a present." Peter handed him a tall triangular bottle.

"Berovian slivovitz," Tomas said. "This brings back memories."

Peter turned to Greta. "My cousin will be here any minute. Then we'll get going."

"All right. I just have to go to the washroom."

"Let's break it open," Tomas said, after Greta walked away. He and Peter disappeared into his office.

"Somebody should tell Greta," Lara said.

"Here's your chance," Alex said as Greta returned from the washroom.

Just then a tall blond woman came through the front door. She looked around hesitantly. "Can I help you?" Lara asked.

"Is Peter Jurak here?" the woman said. She spoke English with a Berovian accent.

Greta walked up to her. "You must be Peter's cousin, Iris. I'm Greta." They shook hands. "Welcome to Vancouver. Peter said you had a rough flight."

"Not so bad."

"You got lucky with the weather. It's usually raining here this time of year."

"We're used to that in Sarno," she said.

Aha, Alex thought. Iris was the woman Boris saw Peter with in Sarno. He wasn't cheating on Greta. He glanced at Lara. She studiously avoided his gaze.

"Lara has something she wants to tell you, Greta," Alex said mischievously.

"What is it?" Greta asked, as Lara cast a dagger glance at Alex.

"It's uh, uh, nothing. Never mind," she said. "It's not important."

"Let's get Peter before he's completely drunk," Greta said to Iris. She led her to Tomas's office, knocked on the door, and walked in without waiting for an answer.

Alex smirked at Lara. She held up her hand. "Don't say a word."

A few minutes after Lara left for her practice the printer's deliveryman arrived with the brochures.

"Where do you want me to put this?" he asked Alex.

"Just put it on the floor by the filing cabinet."

After the guy left, Alex checked out the brochure. *Discover the Greek Islands*, the title read, above a picture of a cruise ship with a beautiful girl in a bikini lying on one of two lounge chairs on the deck. The second chair was empty, the suggestion, of course, being that special perks awaited anyone wise enough to sign up for the cruise. Only a fool would be taken in by something that obvious, Alex thought, but he couldn't stop himself from feeling an intense desire to occupy the empty lounge chair.

He took two brochures out of the carton and brought them into Tomas's office. Tomas and Roman were sitting on the couch in the corner, drinking some of the slivovitz Peter had brought from Berovia.

"The brochures arrived," Alex said. He gave one to Roman and one to Tomas. "Do you still want me to stick around?"

"No. You can go," Roman said.

"Okay," Alex said. "I'll see you next Saturday. Want me to close the door?"

"Leave it open," Tomas said.

Alex went back to his desk to collect his stuff.

"How many are signed up for the presentation?" Roman asked, his voice audible through the open door.

"Sixteen so far."

"You want to run through it with me tomorrow morning before I go to the airport?"

"I'll be fine."

Alex grabbed his knapsack and headed for the front door. He wondered where his uncle was going. The trip must be important if he'd miss a presentation for it.

Alex opened the door and was about to step outside when he realized he'd forgotten his cellphone.

"What time do you land in Rome?" Tomas asked after the door banged shut.

"Ten in the morning, local time. Then it's a three-hour drive to the coast."

Berovia is off the coast of Italy, Alex couldn't help thinking. His phone wasn't on his desk. He looked under the desk and saw it on the floor.

"Is everything set on this end?" Tomas asked.

Alex got down on his knees and reached for his phone.

"Yes. They're doing the operation on Friday."

Operation? What kind of operation? An unwelcome thought crossed Alex's mind.

"Is that the time?" Tomas asked. "We'd better get going or we'll be late for the meeting."

Alex froze on the spot. From his hiding place under the desk he saw two sets of legs head for the door. He waited there for a few minutes after Roman and Tomas left in case they came back. His mind was racing. His uncle was going to the coast of Italy to bring back somebody to Canada for an operation. It couldn't be the Snowman. Could it?

He forced himself to calm down and examine the facts. He knew that his uncle was flying to Rome and then was driving to the coast. That didn't prove anything, he realized. Italy had two coasts. Berovia was off the east coast but maybe Roman was travelling west. If he was, that would put an end to Alex's speculation and put his mind at rest.

He opened his browser. Google Maps would tell him which coast was a three-hour drive from Rome. A quick glance was all it took. Rome was less than fifty miles from the west coast. His uncle was headed east. Alex's heart sank. Then he remembered the plastic surgeon's website he'd seen on Tomas's computer, and his heart sank even further.

Roman and Tomas were helping one of his father's murderers get an operation that would allow him to disappear without a trace—and Alex had less than a week to stop them.

The best opportunity to catch the Snowman would be at the airport when he and Roman arrived in Vancouver, before he had a chance to go into hiding. Alex wondered if his uncle had booked a return flight. He went into Roman's office and turned on his computer. His uncle didn't seem to be too concerned about covering his tracks. The email from Air Canada with his itinerary was sitting in his inbox for all to see. He was returning Tuesday, in three days, at 17:25, airline time for 5:25 p.m. A second passenger was listed on the ticket. Giuseppe Mangano. Alex wondered how they came up with the name.

CHAPTER FIFTEEN

Lara was waiting by her mother's car in the school parking lot Tuesday afternoon when Alex and Stefan arrived. Nobody said much on the twenty-minute drive to the airport. Alex knew they all shared the same hope—that they were somehow wrong about Roman despite the evidence that suggested otherwise.

Lara had been shocked when Alex first told her he suspected that Roman was involved in smuggling the Snowman out of Italy. "I don't believe it," she had said flatly, changing her mind only after grilling Alex at length about the conversation he'd overheard at the travel agency. Stefan was less skeptical. "Nothing a Berovian or a Maldan did would surprise me," he said. "Not when it has something to do with the war. It's impossible to understand unless you grew up there."

Berovian blood ran in Roman's veins, but if he was trying to smuggle Koralic into the country it ran a lot deeper than Alex thought. If he got caught, and Alex was determined to make sure that happened, he would go to jail for a long, long time. He must really believe in his cause if he was willing to take that chance. *This is going to kill Mom*, Alex said to himself, as he pictured Anna's reaction when she learned her brother was trying to protect one of her husband's murderers.

The first thing they did when they got to the airport

was confirm that flight 242 from Rome was arriving on schedule. Then they cased out the arrivals area to find a hiding place where they could stay out of sight but still see the passengers coming through the doors. The pillar near the exit to the baggage claim area was perfect. They had a half hour to kill, so they went to Tim Hortons and ran over their plan one more time.

If Roman and Koralic came through the doors together, all three would follow them to the baggage carousel. If they came through separately, Lara would follow Roman and Stefan would follow Koralic. Koralic might be able to disguise his face but it would be impossible to disguise that body, so in the unlikely event that there were two passengers built like the Snowman, Alex would stay in the arrivals area to make sure both would be followed.

The plan was to confront Koralic before he left the terminal and scream bloody murder until the cops arrived. To help make their case, they had brought numerous photos of the Snowman along with newspaper articles that proved he was wanted by the War Crimes Tribunal.

They returned to their hiding place a few minutes before the plane was due to arrive. Fifteen minutes later Roman came through the arrivals door pushing a wheelchair. The man in the wheelchair had a blanket over his legs and his torso, and he was wearing an oxygen mask that hid half his face.

"Brilliant," Alex whispered with grudging admiration. Lara and Stefan nodded in agreement.

Roman wheeled the man down the left side of the ramp and then stopped.

"What's he waiting for?" Lara whispered. The words were barely out of her mouth when Roman's wife, Sophia, walked through the arrival doors.

What the …? Alex said to himself. As he was trying to make sense of the situation, Sophia bent down and said something to the man in the wheelchair. He took off his oxygen mask to answer her. Alex's first thought, when he saw the emaciated face with sunken cheeks and deep-set eyes, was that Koralic had already undergone plastic surgery. Then he remembered he was having his operation in Vancouver. He stared at the face again. It wasn't the Snowman. Even Peter Jurak couldn't make him up to look like that.

Roman pushed the wheelchair in their direction. Alex, Lara, and Stefan inched around the pillar in order to stay hidden. After the wheelchair passed them, Sophia took a bottle of water out of her bag and handed it to the man in the wheelchair. "Have some water, Grandpa," she said.

Alex and Stefan were back home in time for dinner. Alex felt both better and worse than he had the past few days. It had been a huge relief to find out that his uncle wasn't involved with the Snowman's escape. But the revelation put an end to the hope that his father's murderers would finally be caught.

A casual question to Anna tied up the loose ends. Sophia's grandfather had been living by himself in Italy ever since his wife died a few years earlier. A month ago he had started to experience chest pains. The doctors said he needed to have a bypass operation. Sophia decided to bring him to Canada for the surgery so she could look after him. After the operation he was going to stay in Canada with Sophia and Roman.

Way to go, genius, the Voice said. Alex had been so quick to conclude that Roman was travelling to Italy to get the

Snowman that he hadn't considered any other possibility. If he had, he might have remembered his uncle telling Tomas that Sophia's grandfather wasn't well, and he might have recalled that Sophia had applied for a passport, and then he might have been able to connect the dots and avoid making a complete fool of himself.

"Roman didn't even hesitate when Sophia asked him if her grandfather could live with them. Isn't that something?" Anna continued. "That's how you're supposed to take care of aging relatives. I hope you two will remember that when the time comes," she joked.

Alex just sat there and nodded. Roman was a good man. He'd proven it time and time again. His generosity toward Sophia's grandfather was just another example. How could Alex have believed his uncle was capable of the kind of treachery he'd been so quick to accuse him of? He felt like a complete shit.

CHAPTER SIXTEEN

Alex's initial thought when he woke up the following Saturday was that he would be seeing Roman for the first time since the fiasco. Thank God his uncle would never know what he had suspected him of. Alex felt foolish and embarrassed. The Stork and the Snowman headed Interpol's Most Wanted list. Police agencies all over the world were looking for them. He must have been a lunatic to think that he would beat them to it.

Alex turned his mind to that night's game against Chilliwack. It was Richmond's first game of the regular season. The Cougars had romped to three pre-season victories, and looked impressive doing it. But those games didn't count in the standings, and as far as Alex was concerned, tonight's season opener was the real day one.

Chilliwack was one of the weaker teams in the league but Alex was still nervous. Coach Hampton had given Earl Bales plenty of ice time in the exhibition games, and he had played well enough to prove to all concerned that he was ready to step in if Alex faltered. Alex knew Hampton wasn't going to yank him the first time he made a mistake. But with the team's hopes as high as they were, he wondered how many mistakes he'd be allowed to make. *Not many*, the Voice predicted.

He did his push-ups and sit-ups, put on the University of Minnesota hockey shirt he always wore on game day, and logged on to his computer. A new item came up on the Twitter feed. The Berovian government was upping the reward to $250,000. *Big deal*, Alex thought as he headed downstairs. That wasn't going to make a difference. All it showed was how desperate the government had become.

Anna was sitting at the kitchen table reading the paper. "The interview with you and Stefan," she said, handing him the sports section. It was folded open to the second page. There was a picture of Alex and his brother standing beside each other in their goalie equipment. The headline read: SEPARATED BY WAR, UNITED BY HOCKEY.

Alex sat down and read the article. The reporter pushed all the buttons as she described the tragic circumstances that had separated him and Stefan, and the miraculous way they'd found each other. Then she moved on to hockey. "Asked who was the better goalie, both brothers gave the same media-savvy response: He is. But that debate will be decided on the ice, and the answer may well determine which team wins this year's championship."

Alex could feel his stomach tighten up. The reporter had tapped into a secret fear, one as secret as the fact that he was a virgin—the fear that Stefan was a better goalie than he was. *Fear or knowledge?* asked the Voice. *Knowledge*, Alex admitted. He had known it ever since the game against Team Maldania when Stefan made saves he could only dream of making. It was weird. It didn't bother him a bit then, when Stefan was just some dude from Maldania. Alex had nothing but admiration for the way he played. But Stefan wasn't just some dude from Maldania. He was his brother, and Alex's admiration had turned to jealousy. A classic case of sibling rivalry, he thought, although he seemed to be the only one who was aware of the competition.

"It's a lovely article, isn't it?" Anna said. Alex nodded. Just then Stefan came into the kitchen, rubbing sleep out of his eyes.

"Morning, dude," Anna said. *Now she's calling him dude*, Alex said to himself resentfully. He knew he was being petty but he couldn't help it. He'd had Anna all to himself his entire life. It was going to take more than a month to get used to sharing her.

"Morning," Stefan grunted. *At least he's not calling her Anna.*

"Did you get your chemistry test back?" she asked.

"Yeah," Stefan said. "I got 78."

"That's wonderful." The phone rang. Anna picked it up. "Hello, Boris … I'm fine. How are you? … When do you arrive?"

Stefan perked up. "When's he coming?" he asked, his voice rising with excitement.

"Yes, he's right here," Anna said. She handed the phone to Stefan.

"Hi, Dad," he said in Berovian, his eyes lighting up the way they did every time his father called. "When are you coming? … How long can you stay for? … That's great … Yeah, I got 78 percent …" Stefan started walking out of the kitchen so he could have some privacy. "We play Hollyburn. It's going to be a tough game. They made it to the finals last year, and our top two scorers are injured."

"When's Boris coming?" Alex asked his mother.

"In two weeks. It will be nice for Stefan. He misses him a lot more than he lets on … I've got to go to the store in Abbotsford. Do you need a lift to the travel agency?"

"No. I don't start work until eleven."

"Okay. Good luck tonight. Remember, Stefan and I are meeting you at Lombardo's after the game."

"Okay," Alex said. *How come she's going to his game, not yours?* the Voice asked. Alex pushed away his resentment. Anna had never seen Stefan play, except at the TelCel Cup when she didn't know he was her son. It was only natural that she'd go to his game.

His mom leaned down and kissed the top of his head. "Love you," she said.

"Love you, too." Anna waved goodbye and headed off. There was an extra bounce in her stride. Alex had never seen his mom so happy. He pushed aside the resentment he felt about that, too.

He was eating a bowl of cereal when Stefan came back into the kitchen. "Everything okay?" Alex asked.

"All of it is good," he said cheerfully.

"It's all good," Alex said, correcting him.

"It's all good," Stefan repeated.

"That's great that your dad's coming," Alex said.

"It's fantastic," Stefan said, not trying to hide his excitement like most guys would. His brother came across as someone who took everything in stride, but Alex knew that moving to Vancouver was a bigger adjustment than he let on. As close as he had gotten to Alex, and to Anna, Boris was his anchor, the person who had been there all his life.

"How long is he staying?" Alex asked.

"Two weeks. He'll be here when we play you guys."

"No worries. He's seen you lose before," Alex said with a confidence he didn't feel.

"It's sad to see such a young person lose touch with reality," Stefan said.

Alex laughed. He got to his feet. "I have to go to work. I'll see you at the restaurant after the game."

"What are you doing afterward?"

"Nothing. Why?"

"A friend of Emma's from her dance class is having a party. I'm sure it would be cool if you wanted to come. Lots of good-looking girls will be there."

"Could be fun," Alex said, not committing himself one way or the other. "Good luck tonight."

"You too."

Alex headed out of the kitchen. He thought about warning Stefan about Jamie Balfour, one of Hollyburn's players, but decided against it. *Let him figure it out for himself.* He stopped at the doorway, his better instincts taking over. "Watch out for number 37. He likes to camp out in front of the net. First time he crowds you, whack him on the ankle. He'll back off after that. He acts tough but he's a wuss … A wimp," he explained when he saw that Stefan didn't know what *wuss* meant. "Weak," he explained again when he realized Stefan didn't know what *wimp* meant either.

"Number 37?" Stefan asked, making sure he had it right.

"Yeah. All right. Later, bro."

"Later."

"Alex," Roman called out from the doorway to his office. "I need a copy of the passenger list for the Greek Island tour."

"Just printing it up now," Alex said.

Lara was on the phone. "I'll mail the tickets to you right away… My pleasure …"

"Want to go to the new Jet Li movie tonight?" she asked Alex after she hung up. Alex wondered why Lara wasn't seeing Jason on a Saturday night, but he wasn't about to ask. *Maybe she's come to her senses and dumped him.*

"Jason's cousins are in from Calgary and he's got a family dinner," Lara continued. *Or not.*

"Can't," Alex said with a regretful shrug. "I got a game and then I'm having dinner with Mom and Stefan. What about tomorrow afternoon?"

It was Lara's turn to shrug. "I got practice."

"When's the tournament?"

"In three weeks."

"Is Tonya competing this year?"

"Yup." Tonya Livingstone had defeated Lara in the provincial muay Thai finals the year before. Lara would have to beat her this time in order to achieve her goal of making it to the national championships.

"You're going to dust her," Alex said confidently. Lara shrugged, unconvinced. "All that hard work will pay off. You'll see." Lara worked out two hours a day, five days a week. He'd gone to one of her workouts. It made hockey practice look like a walk in the park.

Alex took the passenger list out of the printer tray and went into his uncle's office. Roman and Tomas were in mid-conversation.

"A $250,000 reward," Tomas said to Roman in disgust. "I knew this government would be a disaster, but I didn't know they'd be this bad. They should give a medal of honor to Zarkov and Koralic instead of pulling this shit."

Alex couldn't believe his ears. "What did you say?" he said angrily. Roman and Tomas turned around. "Those two men murdered my father and you want to give them a medal? Are you out of your freaking mind?"

"What are you talking about?" Tomas asked.

"Alex's father died at San Marco," Roman explained.

"He didn't die. Zarkov and Koralic murdered him," Alex said.

"I'm sorry about what happened to your father," Tomas said. "But we didn't start the war. The Maldans did." It was a debatable statement, but Alex wasn't in the mood for a debate.

"What did San Marco have to do with the war? The people in the church weren't soldiers."

"They had to do something. The Maldans were slaughtering every Berovian they could lay their hands on."

"And that makes it okay to burn innocent people alive?" Alex said furiously.

"That's enough," Roman said.

Tomas ignored him. "All they did was stand up for their country. They're heroes."

Alex rushed at Tomas, his arm cocked, but before he could get to him, Roman stepped in front of Alex and wrapped his arms around him. "You're a fucking asshole," Alex yelled at Tomas. He tried to get free but Roman had him in a vice grip.

"Tomas, go to your office," Roman ordered.

Tomas left, glaring at Alex, who glared right back at him.

"Let me go," Alex said to Roman.

"Not until you calm down."

"I'm calm." Roman's eyes searched Alex's and then, satisfied, he released him.

"What the hell do you think you're doing?" Roman asked.

"You're taking his side? You agree with him?"

"No, I don't," Roman said firmly. "Zarkov and Koralic are war criminals and they should pay for what they've done. But that doesn't excuse your behavior. I'm trying to run a business here. I can't have people running around acting like a bunch of lunatics."

"So he's allowed to just go around saying stuff like that?" Alex said indignantly. "I can't believe you're going to let him get away with it. You should fire his ass."

"I can't fire somebody for his political beliefs unless they interfere with the business. But what I can do, and what I will do, is read him the riot act and tell him that if he brings the subject up again here in the office, he'll lose his job. I can't do more than that." He looked at Alex, seeking confirmation that he was being fair.

"That's bullshit," Alex said, not giving it to him. "Either he goes or I go."

"I'll pretend I didn't hear that. You need to settle down. Take the rest of the day off and think about it."

Alex walked out of the office without saying anything. He didn't have to think about it. There was no way he was going to work with that prick. Tomas was sitting at his desk. Alex stopped at the doorway.

"Alex," Roman warned from the hallway.

Alex gave Tomas the finger and continued on to the front door.

"What's wrong?" Lara asked as he passed her.

Alex put his hand up to indicate he couldn't talk. He walked out of the office and headed down Main Street, oblivious to his surroundings, his emotions in an uproar. His phone rang. He saw that it was Lara but he was too agitated to talk.

A half hour later he was all the way downtown with no recollection of getting there. He went into a coffee shop at the corner of Main and East Pender. He wasn't going to quit, he decided. He wouldn't give Tomas the satisfaction and besides, where was he going to find another boss who would give him time off whenever he needed it? But if Tomas said another good word about Zarkov and Koralic, he was going to clock him.

His phone rang again. This time he answered.

"Are you okay?" Lara asked in a concerned voice.

"I'm fine."

"What happened? … I can't believe Tomas is such a moron," she said after he told her. "How can anybody think those horrible men are heroes?"

"He's not the only one," Alex said. "That's why they haven't been caught yet." And if things kept going the way they were, they never would.

CHAPTER SEVENTEEN

Alex was hungry enough to eat a horse by the time Kenny
Nelson dropped him off at Lombardo's after the game
against Chilliwack.

"Great game, Alex. You were fantastic, man," Kenny
said as Alex got out of the car. "We would have lost
without you."

"Thanks. See you tomorrow," Alex said.

Alex walked into the restaurant with a bounce in his
stride. Richmond had defeated a surprisingly pesky
Chilliwack team 3–0, but the game was a lot closer than the
score indicated. The Cougars came out flat at the start of
the game, and if Alex hadn't been as sharp as he was—
turning aside three legitimate scoring opportunities in the
first five minutes—the Condors would have grabbed an
early lead that could have changed the outcome.

Coach Hampton singled out Alex for praise in the
locker room after the game. "You guys talk about winning
the championship, but I didn't see anything resembling a
championship team out there tonight," he said. "A fifty-
minute effort in a sixty-minute game isn't going to get it
done. Alex was the only man in this locker room who was
ready to play from the opening face-off." He slowly looked
around the room to make sure everyone got the point.

Alex's teammates were equally appreciative. Even Earl
Bales congratulated him, although Alex knew that didn't

mean Bales had stopped hoping that Alex would screw up so he could replace him as the starting goalie. *Fair enough*, Alex thought. Earl could hope all he wanted, but if Alex kept playing the way he was, he just might be wearing a University of Minnesota uniform before Bales got his chance.

Stefan and Anna came into the restaurant. "How was your game, sweetie?" Anna asked as they sat down at the table.

"Good. We won 3–0."

"That's great," Stefan said.

"How did you guys do?" Alex asked.

"We won 1–0."

"You should have seen your brother," Anna said. "He was fantastic."

Alex felt the air go out of him. He pasted a smile on his face. "Way to go, bro," he said.

"Isn't that amazing?" Anna said. "You both got shutouts." *Yeah*, the Voice said, *except yours came against one of the worst teams in the league and his came against one of the best.*

"Thanks for the tip about number 37," Stefan said. "I hit him the first time he came in the crease and he didn't bother me again. He's a wiss, just like you said."

"A wuss."

"A wuss."

"I won't bother asking if there's going to be alcohol at the party," Anna said to Stefan when they arrived at the house. "I was seventeen once."

"Really?" Alex asked, with fake disbelief.

Anna ignored him. "But if you're going to take the car you have to promise that you won't have anything to drink," she continued. Anna was fanatical about drinking and driving. Every time there was an article in the paper about an accident where alcohol played a role, she was sure to bring it to their attention.

"Yes, Mom," Stefan said patiently. It was the third time she'd told him since they'd left the restaurant. "You sure you don't want to come?" he asked Alex. "Emma's friend said it would be cool."

"I'm going to take a pass," Alex said. "I got a ton of homework to do."

Homework wasn't the real reason he didn't want to go. He just didn't feel like going to a party where he wouldn't know anybody. He knew from past experience that he'd just stand around feeling like a dork.

Alex was playing on his computer when heard Stefan come up the stairs.

"Hey," Stefan said from the doorway.

"Hey. How was the party?"

"You didn't miss anything. Just a bunch of people drinking and acting stupid."

"Don't they do that in Maldania?"

"Some people do. I don't hang out with them." *He has absolutely no interest in being cool*, Alex thought. Maybe that's why he *is* so cool. "We cut out early and went over to Emma's place."

"You two are seeing a lot of each other. Things must be going good," Alex said, hoping Stefan would provide some details. Like whether or not he and Emma were having sex. He was pretty sure they were, although if that was the case, his brother wasn't bragging about it. "Good," was all he would say when Alex asked how things were going with Emma.

The guy's been here for less than a month and he's hooking up with a fox like Emma, Alex said to himself enviously. Meanwhile he was … *going steady with your right hand,* the Voice suggested helpfully. Alex and Stefan had talked about pretty much everything, but the one thing they hadn't talked about was sex, other than joke about it like guys did. As close as he felt to Stefan, he wasn't about to admit that he'd never had sex. That was something he was determined to … *take to your grave?* the Voice suggested again.

Alex was about to fall asleep when his phone beeped with a text message from Lara.

You up?

Yup, he texted back.

You okay?

He knew she was referring to his fight with Tomas. *I'm good. Tomas is a dick.*

The biggest … did you win?

Beat Chilliwack 3–0.

They must really suck.

Good night.

Nite. See you Monday. Sleep well.

You too … and thanks.

Lara's a good friend, he thought. He hoped Jason knew how lucky he was. *I dare you to say that with a straight face,* the Voice said.

CHAPTER EIGHTEEN

Alex swung his legs over the side of the bed. As soon as his feet hit the floor, he felt a sharp stabbing pain in his ankle, but it disappeared by the time he got to his desk and logged on to his computer to get the latest league results. In the two weeks since the win over Chilliwack, Richmond had won three more games. West Van had kept pace, leaving the two teams tied for first place with identical 4–0 records. Hollyburn was in third with a 3–1 record. Early days, but it was shaping up to be a three-way contest for the league championship.

Alex was having a great season, his best ever, but Stefan had been even better. West Van's top two scorers had been injured all season, and the fact that the Lightning were still undefeated was mainly due to his outstanding play.

On Thursday, two days from now, Richmond and West Van would face off against each other for the first time this season. Alex was nervous at the prospect of going up against his brother. He hated feeling this way but he was powerless to prevent it.

He did his push-ups and sit-ups, got dressed and went downstairs. Anna had left a note on the kitchen table for him and Stefan. "There are clean sheets for the sofa bed in my office. Please make the bed before Boris arrives." Boris was arriving that afternoon to visit Stefan.

A few seconds later Stefan limped into the kitchen. "What happened to you?" Alex asked.

"I took a puck on the ankle in practice yesterday," Stefan said.

"You weren't limping last night."

"I know. It didn't hurt until I got out of bed."

That stupid question Alex had been asked about whether twins felt each other's pain didn't seem so stupid now.

"That's freaky," Alex said. He told Stefan about the pain in his ankle when he got out of bed.

"Freaky," his brother agreed.

"How does it feel?" Alex asked.

"Pretty sore. I've got a physio appointment after school. I hope I'll be able to play on Thursday."

"Me, too," Alex said. *Yeah, right*, said the Voice. Alex held up Anna's note. "Mom wants you to make the bed before Boris arrives. The bedding is in her office."

"Nice try, bro," Stefan said. "I already saw the note."

"Rock, paper, scissors?" Alex asked. Stefan nodded.

"Two out of three?" Stefan asked after Alex's paper wrapped up his rock.

"Don't forget to tuck in the sheets," Alex said.

"That's a lot better," Alex said to Earl Bales. "Now try it in the other direction." He lobbed a shot at Bales from the face-off circle. Earl caught the puck and put it on the ice, and then stickhandled it in a counter-clockwise figure eight around the two orange pylons Alex had set up in front of the goal.

Alex had been helping Earl since the start of the season, answering all his questions and working with him after practice. Even though he knew the rookie wanted his job, Bales was his teammate and, as Lou Roberts would have put it, a member of the clan, and Alex felt it was his duty to help him. If Earl had been a dick it might have been a different story, but he was a good guy who never gave Alex any attitude. He just wanted to get better and he was smart enough to know Alex could help him do it.

Their teammates were sitting around in various stages of undress when they got back to the locker room. Neil Daniels was walking around the room handing out bottles of water. Mike Leonard took a bottle and then grabbed Neil's glasses off his face.

Neil reached for them. Leonard held them over his head, out of his reach. "Give them back," Neil said.

Leonard stuck them in his jockstrap. "Come and get them," he said. Once again half the team laughed while the other half, including Alex, looked around sheepishly. A couple of seconds later Leonard took the glasses out of his jock, held them to his nose as if he were holding a fine cigar, and gave an exaggerated sniff of appreciation.

"Oooh," everybody said in disgust.

Leonard tossed the glasses to Neil. Neil caught them, and holding them by the tip of one arm, hurried to the washroom to clean them off.

"Soap and water aren't going to do the job, Pie," Stevie Ryan called after him. "Those things need to be fumigated after where they've been."

"Your sister isn't complaining," Mike said.

Stevie gave him the finger. Leonard laughed good-naturedly.

Alex caught Kenny Nelson's eye. Kenny shrugged. Alex knew Kenny felt the same way about Leonard that he did. So did a lot of the other guys. But as usual, none of them said anything. They were all afraid Leonard would turn on them if they did. Leonard was six three and weighed over two hundred pounds. Fear was a perfectly logical feeling.

"Are you and Stefan going to play guitar for us?" Anna asked Boris when dinner was finished.

"What do you say?" Boris asked Stefan.

"Let's do it."

They all went into the living room. Alex and Anna sat down on the couch. Boris and Stefan sat on chairs in front of them. It was obvious from the moment they started playing that they had played together a lot, and that they had a lot of fun doing it. After a few bars Anna started singing along. Alex had never heard her sing in Berovian before.

"That was wonderful," Anna said when the song came to an end.

"You have a lovely voice," Boris told her.

"I'm surprised I remembered the words. It's been a long time."

"I bet you know this one, too," Boris said, starting in on another song.

As Alex watched Boris and Stefan play, he was conscious of feeling a profound sense of loss. It was no knock against Anna, she was the greatest, but there were things a boy could only get from his father. It was a lot more than having somebody to teach you how to play guitar, or to shoot the puck at you. It was hard to put it into words. A father showed a son how to be a man. He knew that was vague, but it was the best he could come up with. Stefan had Boris to show him how to be a man. He didn't have anyone.

They played folk songs for an hour or so, with Anna

singing along to most of them, before Boris finally put his guitar down.

"My fingers are going to feel it tomorrow," he said. "I haven't played this much since Stefan left."

"Me neither," Stefan said.

"That brought back a lot of memories," Anna said. "Darko and I used to listen to those songs all the time." She stared off into space. "I've got to do some work," she said a few moments later. "I'll see you all in the morning."

Stefan picked up his guitar after Anna left the room. He gave his father a questioning glance. Boris shook his head. Stefan started playing, challenging his father with a look. Boris grabbed his guitar and soon the two were off in their own world.

He and his brother were like flip sides of the same coin, Alex thought. He grew up without a father; Stefan grew up without a mother. Except now Stefan had a mother and he would never have a father, Alex thought bitterly. He could feel his anger at the Stork and the Snowman rise up. They had murdered his father and separated him and his brother. They had ripped his family apart, changed all their lives forever. If this was a movie, Alex knew how it would end. He would track them down and blow their freaking heads off. Too bad things like that never happened in real life.

CHAPTER NINETEEN

Anna and Boris were chatting over coffee when Alex walked into the kitchen two days later.

"Morning, dude," Anna said. "How did you sleep?"

"I've slept better," he said. He never slept well the night before a game, but he was extra nervous about tonight's game against West Van.

Anna laughed. "Thinking about the game?"

"Would you believe me if I said no?"

"Absolutely," Anna said. "Not."

A minute later Stefan walked into the kitchen. "Morning, dude," Anna said.

"Morning," Stefan grunted.

"How's the ankle?" Boris asked.

"It's all better," Stefan said.

"Will you be able to play tonight?" Anna asked.

"Definitely," Stefan said. He glanced at Boris, who had a skeptical look on his face. Stefan ran on the spot for a few strides without a grimace. He looked at his dad again. "It feels great."

"Wonderful," Anna said.

"Jump up and touch the ceiling," Boris said.

Stefan crouched and jumped. The moment he left the floor his face contorted in pain. Two seconds after he landed a dejected look replaced the pained one. He wasn't ready to play and he knew it. Alex knew how much Stefan

wanted to play, especially since Boris was here, but at the
same time as he shared his brother's disappointment—
Yeah, I can tell you're all choked up about it, the Voice said—he
had to admit that he was a bit relieved. He would have to
face his fears sooner or later, but with the way he was
feeling right now, later would suit him just fine.

"It's only one game," Boris said. "Better to miss one
game now than a bunch of games later. Stay off it for a
couple of days and you'll be fine for the game against
Langley on Wednesday."

"But you're not going to be here on Wednesday,"
Stefan said. Boris was taking the red-eye to Maldania after
the game that night. He'd been forced to cut his trip short
to attend the funeral of a friend who had died after a long
illness.

"I know. I'm disappointed, too. But I'll be back in
December and I'll see you play then."

"That's more than two months from now," Stefan said.
He bent his knees and pushed off his sore ankle as if it
might have healed in the past two minutes, but the wince
on his face showed there had been no miracle cure.

The school day seemed to go on forever, as it always did on
game day. Alex sat in biology class trying, unsuccessfully, to
pay attention to Mr. Drake as he tried, just as
unsuccessfully, to excite the class about synthetic enzymes.
Drake was a good teacher, but it was the last class of the
day and after enduring two straight weeks of grey skies,
everybody was itching to get outside and enjoy a rare warm
and sunny afternoon.

"Don't forget," Drake said when the bell finally rang,
"your assignments are due tomorrow." Everybody groaned.

Alex decided to go the library and finish his

assignment. It was next to impossible to do homework before a game, but completely impossible to do any after. Doing it now was the lesser of two evils. He stopped by Stefan's locker to tell him he wouldn't be going home with him. His brother wasn't there yet. Alex was debating whether to wait for him when a pair of hands hugged him from behind. "Hey, handsome," a voice whispered. The warm breath in his ear sent a shiver down his spine. He turned around.

"I'm sorry," Emma said, taking a quick step backward. Her face was red with embarrassment. "I thought you were Stefan," she added unnecessarily.

I wish I was, Alex couldn't stop himself from thinking. "I figured that out," he said. She laughed.

"Hey, guys," Stefan said as he limped up to them. "Ready to go?" he asked Emma. She nodded. "We're going to hang out at the park," Stefan said. "Want to join us?"

"Don't you have a chemistry test tomorrow?"

"I've got it under control," Stefan said.

Like everything else, Alex thought. "I'm glad someone does. I have an assignment to finish. I'll see you at home later."

"What time do we have to leave for the game?"

"Six. Mom's picking Boris up at the travel agency and then she'll come get us." Alex turned to Emma. "You still coming to dinner tomorrow?"

"Yeah. I'm sorry I won't get a chance to meet your dad," she said to Stefan.

Alex headed to the library. He stopped before turning the corner and looked back. Stefan and Emma were standing by his locker, holding hands and looking into each other's eyes as if nobody else in the universe existed. The only person who'd ever looked at him that way was Anna, and he only knew that because he'd seen his baby pictures in the photo album. *Come to think of it, she could have been looking at Stefan*, he thought.

Richmond dominated West Vancouver from start to finish, and by the time the final buzzer sounded, the scoreboard read Cougars 4, Lightning 1.

The mood in the locker room was euphoric. The win had kept the team's undefeated streak intact and given it undisputed ownership of first place in the league.

"Great game, Alex," Doug Harvey said.

"Thanks." Alex had played another strong game, but he knew he'd have faced a tougher test if Stefan had been in the net for West Van. The Lightning's backup goaltender let in a couple of easy goals in the first period and his teammates played tentatively after that, reluctant to take any chances on the offensive end in case they gave Richmond a scoring opportunity. Alex had been sharp when he had to be, but it had been a relatively easy night.

"Man, we creamed them," Harvey crowed.

"Feels good," shouted Terry Gilliam.

"Almost as good as sex," Jeremy Westover said, clapping Alex on the shoulder. "Right, buddy?"

"Not if you're doing it right," Alex said. Everybody in hearing distance laughed.

"Nice win, gentlemen, but don't let it go to your head," Coach Hampton said as he walked into the room. "We beat a wounded team tonight. West Van was missing their starting goalie and their two best offensive players. That's not the team you're going to meet in the playoffs, so I suggest you hold back on ordering the championship ring. We've got a lot of hard work ahead of us."

His assessment pretty much summed up the way Alex

looked at it. It was nice to win but the victory didn't mean much. West Van would be a different team when his brother was back between the pipes.

"I'm turning in," Anna said as she walked into Alex's bedroom. He was playing the hockey video game Stefan had given him. "Make sure Stefan locks the door when he gets in." Stefan had taken Boris to the airport after the game so he could catch his flight back to Maldania.

"I will."

"You played a great game tonight, honey."

"Thanks, Mom."

Alex was still playing the game a half hour later when he heard Stefan come upstairs. He expected him to come in and say hello but Stefan went straight to his room and started playing his guitar. It was one of the songs he and Boris had played, one of the sad ones. Alex got out of bed and went into his brother's room. Stefan stopped playing.

"You okay?" Alex asked.

"I'm good." He started playing again.

Alex plopped down on a chair in the corner of the room. A framed enlargement of the photo Stefan had taken of the two of them at the top of Whistler hung on one wall. A collage of photos from Stefan's life in Maldania was pinned on a bulletin board on another wall, with pictures of Stefan from the time he was a little boy. They reminded Alex of the different lives they had lived before they met, and of all the years that had been lost.

When the song ended Alex got to his feet. "Good night."

"Good night."

He walked out of the room. As soon as he closed the door, Stefan started playing another song. Another sad one.

CHAPTER TWENTY

The following weekend was a long weekend—Monday was a teachers' professional development day—but Alex had all his homework done by noon on Saturday. He had stayed home Friday night and gotten up early that morning to finish it. That was the deal he and Anna made in exchange for her allowing him to work the rest of the weekend at the travel agency. Roman had three tours leaving in the next week and needed all the help he could get.

Alex put his books away and put on his jogging shoes. He didn't have to be at the travel agency until two. He was on his way out the door when Roman called.

"Can you come in early? I'm having trouble with my computer. I can send out my emails but I'm not receiving any … and yes, I tried restarting it," he added quickly before Alex could ask.

"No problem. I'll be there as soon as I can," Alex said. He'd go for a run later. *It's going to be a profitable weekend*, he thought happily. He could almost hear the Vespa purring.

Lara was at her desk when Alex arrived.

"I didn't know you were working today," he said.

"Sorry. I forgot to clear it with you."

"Sarcasm is the lowest form of humor," Alex said, shaking his head in mock disappointment. "Why didn't Roman get you to fix his computer?"

"I tried. Couldn't figure it out."

"It's a man's job."

"Why don't you give it a shot anyway?" Lara said with a smirk.

Roman was talking to Tomas when Alex walked into his office.

"Thanks for coming in," Roman said. He got out of his chair so Alex could sit down at the computer.

Alex and Tomas gave each other the same hostile stare they'd been exchanging in the three weeks since their fight, but neither said a word. The two of them had reached an uneasy truce. They spoke to each other only when it was an absolute necessity, and Roman had reorganized the chain of command to keep that at a minimum. Whenever Tomas needed anything, he was to call on Lara. Roman had followed through on his promise to lay down the law to Tomas and it apparently had done the trick. Tomas hadn't said another word about the Stork or the Snowman, at least not when Alex was around, and as long as he did that, Alex would keep up his end of the bargain.

"I know Boris is busy, but it's a mistake to wait until January to do a second tour," Tomas said, resuming a conversation Alex had obviously interrupted. "Someone else can lead the tour. We need to strike while the iron is hot."

Alex sat down in front of the computer and went to work.

"Boris said he doesn't have anyone he can trust," Roman said.

"We know people in Berovia. We can find somebody."

"What's the problem? Lina's school bills adding up?"

"It doesn't end with the tuition. They ding you for everything. But that's not the reason I want to move on this. We've got some momentum. We need to take advantage of it."

"It's not going to happen," Roman said.

Tomas held his hands up in mock surrender, an unhappy look on his face, and walked out of the office.

Alex saw that Roman's inbox was full. He increased the inbox capacity and sent out a test mail. "You're good to go," he said to Roman when it arrived.

"What did you do?" Roman asked. "Never mind, I wouldn't understand." He handed a folder to Alex. "Give this to Tomas. Think you can do that without starting World War III?"

Alex nodded. He took the folder and walked out of the office. Lara was about to leave for muay Thai practice. "Did you fix it?" she asked.

"What do you think?" Alex said, as if it was the most ridiculous question ever. He flexed, mimicking a bodybuilder's pose.

"I think you're goofy. But cute. What did you do?"

"It's way too complicated to explain to a girl."

"I take back the bit about you being cute."

Alex was working on a comeback but Lara was out the door before he could think of one. He went into Tomas's office. Tomas was on the phone, his back to the door. "Tell Esteban I called about the passport," he said in Berovian. Alex knocked on the doorframe. Tomas swiveled around in his chair. "I'll call you back," he said abruptly as soon as he saw Alex. He had a guilty look on his face, a very guilty look.

"You think Tomas is trying to get a passport for Koralic?" Stefan asked after Alex told him about the conversation he overheard in Tomas's office. They were in the living room, about to watch the Canucks game against the New York Rangers.

"I'm not going to jump to any conclusions, not after what happened with Roman, but he's up to something. That's for sure. You should have seen the look on his face when he realized I heard him on the phone."

"If the Snowman is still in Italy, he'll need a passport to get out of the country," Stefan reasoned. "And if he's here he'll need one to get out."

"And don't forget about the plastic surgeon's website I saw on Tomas's computer," Alex said. "The one for Lina's nonexistent nose job."

"That doesn't prove anything."

"I know. But you've got to admit it's pretty suspicious."

"Who's Tomas getting the passport from?" Stefan asked.

"Some guy named Esteban."

"Esteban?" Alex nodded. "What did Tomas say exactly?"

"*Birud Esteban bosni passaporta.* 'Tell Esteban I called about the passport.'"

Stefan had a stunned look on his face. "Say that again," he said.

"Tell Esteban I called about the passport."

"No. In Berovian."

"*Birud Esteban bosni passaporta.*"

Stefan stared at him, wide-eyed. "He didn't say *Birud Esteban.* He said *Birud Desteban.*"

"Big deal. So his name is Desteban."

"*Desteban* isn't a name. It's slang—for a fat man."

CHAPTER TWENTY-ONE

Alex and Stefan were waiting outside SpyZone when the doors opened at ten o'clock Sunday morning.

It was part of the plan they'd come up with the night before, a plan based on the assumption—although prayer might be a more accurate description—that Tomas would lead them to the Snowman. The first part of the plan—not to let Tomas out of their sight—was already underway. Lara had driven to his house early that morning so she could follow him wherever he went. She'd already texted Alex to tell him that he'd gone straight to the travel agency.

A middle-aged man wearing a bowtie was behind the counter. "How can I help you boys?" he asked.

"We want the voice-activated pen recorder," Alex said. They'd seen it on the store's website. It cost $139 plus tax. That would delay the Vespa delivery date by a few weeks, but it was a small price to pay if it led to the capture of the Snowman.

The salesman unlocked a display case and took out a box. "You know that it's illegal to record a conversation without the permission of one of the parties," he said as he opened it.

"We know that," Alex lied. "It's for a school project." The words sounded stupid the moment they came out of his mouth but the salesman didn't challenge him.

"It's very simple to use," he said. "You push the clip

down to record. And then use the cable to plug it into your computer when you want to listen. It also works as a pen in case anybody gets suspicious." He showed them how it worked.

"We'll take it," Alex said.

"A school project?" Stefan said when they walked out of the store. "That's the best reason you could think of?"

"I didn't hear you come up with anything," Alex said. "Anyway, he didn't care why we wanted it. He was just covering his ass."

"Covering his ass?" Stefan asked.

"It means making sure he won't get into trouble if we use it illegally." Which, of course, was exactly what they had in mind.

The door to Tomas's office was closed when Alex arrived at the travel agency.

"Did you get it?" Lara asked. Alex nodded. "Cool," she said after he showed her how the pen worked.

The minutes ticked by slowly as Alex waited for Tomas to leave his office so he could plant the pen. His eyes were riveted on the door, willing it to open. Twenty minutes later Tomas came out and went into the washroom. Alex jumped to his feet and raced into his office. He turned the recorder on and put the pen in the cup where Tomas stored his pens and pencils. He was back at his desk in less than a minute.

Tomas came out of the washroom and returned to his office, closing the door behind him. Alex could hear him on the phone but couldn't make out what he was saying. He imagined that every call was the one that would lead to the Snowman. An hour later Tomas emerged, wearing his coat. "I'll be back after lunch," he said to Lara. "If anyone needs me they can get me on my cell."

As soon as Tomas walked out the door, Alex got to his feet. Lara handed him the keys to her mother's car. "Stefan or I will call you if there's anything on the tape," she said. Lara was going to listen to the English telephone conversations. If there were any in Berovian, she'd send the files to Stefan.

Alex followed Tomas north on Main Street, making sure to keep a few vehicles between them. There weren't all that many red Honda Elements in Vancouver and Tomas knew that Lara's mother drove one of them.

Tomas turned right on East 12th and then left on Commercial Drive. Just after he passed East 3rd, he pulled over and parked. Alex did likewise a block back. Tomas got out of his car, crossed the street, and went into a Greek restaurant.

Alex walked to the restaurant. He pulled his baseball cap down over his forehead, raised the collar of his jacket, and cautiously peeked through the window. His heart was beating a mile a minute. He quickly glanced around the restaurant. Tomas was seated at a table in the corner, his back, thankfully, to the door. A man with black hair brushed straight back and a bushy moustache sat across from him.

Alex went back to the car and waited for Tomas to come out. A couple of minutes later, Lara called. "Where are you?" she asked.

"Outside a restaurant, waiting for Tomas. What's up?"

"He's meeting somebody about the passport," she said, unable to control her excitement. "I just listened to the phone call he made before he left the office. He told whoever he was talking to that they were ready to move ahead. The guy told him to bring the money and the photos. And to make sure the photos were the right size," she added meaningfully. *That clinches it*, Alex thought. He and Lara both knew from working at the travel agency that passport photos had to be a specific size. "Then Tomas said he was leaving right away and would see the guy soon."

"He's seeing him right now." He told her about the man in the restaurant.

"Roman asked where you were. I told him you went to get new straps for your goalie pads."

"That was smart." Just then Tomas walked out of the restaurant, alone. "I gotta go," Alex said. "Tomas just left the restaurant. I'll call you later."

"Be careful," she said.

Alex followed Tomas as he drove back up Commercial Drive and turned right onto East 12th. When he made a left on Main, Alex assumed he was going back to the travel agency, but instead he made a right on East 13th and turned into the parking lot of Saint Patrick's Catholic Church. Alex didn't know what to make of that. Tomas was Catholic, but he went to the Berovian Orthodox Church on Hastings along with the rest of the Berovian Mafia. Alex drove past the entrance to the parking lot and pulled over to the curb farther down the road. He got out of the car and hid behind one of the trees that lined the side of the road. Tomas was standing by his car, smoking a cigarette.

Just then Alex's phone rang. It was Stefan. "You're not going to believe this," he said. He was as excited as Lara had been. "I just listened to a call Tomas made. He told the guy on the other end of the phone to pick up some slivovitz for 'our guest,' and to get the best stuff he could find."

He didn't have to explain. Slivovitz was a thoughtful gift for a guest who was visiting from Berovia. And you'd want to get the best stuff if your guest was someone special. Someone like the Snowman.

"Hard to believe, isn't it?" Stefan asked.

Alex was still thinking about how hard it was to believe after Stefan hung up, when a taxi turned into the parking lot and pulled up beside Tomas's car. A man got out of the back seat of the taxi and into the passenger seat of Tomas's car. Alex only saw him from behind. He wore one of those hats you see in old black-and-white movies, the kind with a brim all around, and he was fat. Very fat. Alex warned himself not to let his imagination run away with him. The warning went unheeded.

Alex crept closer to the parking lot, using the parked cars for cover. He hid behind a large recycling bin near the entrance and carefully peeked out. The vantage point gave him an unobstructed view of the fat man sitting in Tomas's car but he was too far away to see his face. Using the camera on his phone, he zoomed in as close as he could, but all he could see was that the man wore sunglasses and the front of his hat was tilted down—as if he didn't want anybody to see his face. Alex snapped a couple of pictures. His stomach was churning like it did before a big game. What had seemed hard to believe a couple of minutes ago suddenly didn't seem so hard to believe. *If that's the Snowman, how did he manage to get into the country?* Alex asked himself. *And how long has he been here?* Then he realized it didn't matter how or when he arrived. The only thing that mattered was making sure he didn't leave.

Alex was wondering just how he was going to manage that when the fat man got out of Tomas's car and got back into the taxi. Alex raced back to his car. As he jumped behind the wheel he saw the taxi drive out of the parking lot and turn right on Main Street. Tomas followed. Alex sped after them. When Tomas passed East 20th, he pulled into a parking spot across from the travel agency. Alex shielded his face with his hand as he passed Tomas's car and prayed that Tomas wasn't looking his way.

He followed the taxi up Main Street. Just before they got to Marine Drive a Canada Post delivery truck pulled out into traffic and cut in between Alex and the taxi. As the taxi went through the intersection, the mail truck signaled for a right turn. It stopped at the corner to allow a few pedestrians to cross the road, forcing Alex to stop as well. He glanced in his side-view mirror but the steady flow of traffic in the passing lane kept him stuck behind the mail truck.

A gap in the passing lane opened up just as the light turned amber. Alex pulled around the mail truck and booted it through the intersection. A block later he was back in position behind the taxi.

He was thanking his lucky stars when a police siren wailed. Alex looked in the rear-view mirror. A cop car was right behind him. The roof light bar was flashing, and the driver was gesturing for him to pull over.

"Fuuuuuuck!" Alex screamed at the top of his lungs. He pulled over to the side of the road, pounding the steering wheel in frustration as the taxi drove out of sight.

A sharp rap on the window summoned his attention. Alex rolled the window down.

"What's the rush, son?" the policeman asked.

Alex wondered what he would do if Alex told him. Probably put him in the loony bin and throw away the key.

"Driver's license and registration, please."

The cop didn't show Alex any mercy. He dinged him

for running the light and for illegally passing the mail truck. Four demerit points and $276 in fines. He'd be lucky to have the Vespa by the time school ended, but that paled beside the bitterness of knowing that the Snowman had slipped through his fingers.

Alex drove back to the agency cursing his bad luck. He was in a foul mood when he walked through the door.

"What took you so long?" Roman asked. He was standing by the filing cabinet with Tomas. "You've been gone for over an hour."

It took Alex a moment to remember his excuse. "Uh … the store on Oak Street didn't have the straps for my pads so I … uh … I had to go out to Burnaby," he said. Tomas gave him a curious look.

"You know better than to leave without asking," Roman said. "Especially since we're so busy."

"I'm sorry. I wasn't thinking."

"That's an understatement."

Alex sat down at his desk. When he glanced up a few moments later, Tomas was still looking at him.

"It's got to be him," Stefan said. Alex and Lara nodded in agreement. They were sitting in Alex's room, comparing the photos Alex took of the fat man sitting in Tomas's car to an online photo of the Snowman.

Even though they couldn't make a positive identification—all they could tell was that the face of the man in Tomas's car was roughly the same shape as the Snowman's—when you put that together with the passport, the plastic surgeon's website on Tomas's computer, and the slivovitz for an honored guest, it all added up.

"We have to find him before he gets his passport," Alex said. "Once he has the operation, he'll leave the country as soon as soon he gets it. And then we'll never find him."

"He might already have had the operation," Stefan said.

"I don't think he's had it," Lara said. "If I was Koralic I'd want to change the shape of my face and it would take months to recover from that. His face would still be bandaged."

"Is there any way we can find out who the plastic surgeon is?" Stefan asked.

"It's got to be somebody local," Alex said. He flipped open his computer. "How many can there be?"

"More than you think," Lara said.

She was right. According to Google there were fifty-six plastic surgeons in the Lower Mainland.

"Tomas must have been in contact with him in order to make all the arrangements," Alex said.

"Or her," said Lara.

"Or her. We need to get on Tomas's computer," Alex said.

"And just how do you plan on doing that?" Stefan asked.

CHAPTER TWENTY-TWO

"I have to leave at four today," Lara said to Roman when he strolled into the travel agency the next day. "I've got practice."

"Me, too," Alex said.

"That's the kind of communication I was talking about yesterday," Roman joked.

Alex and Lara were both lying. Her practice didn't start until six, and he didn't have one. The lies were part of a plan that would, fingers crossed, allow Alex to get on Tomas's computer at the end of the day. Meanwhile, Stefan was waiting at the café across the street so he could follow Tomas if he left the office. They had all the bases covered. Or so they hoped.

Tomas was on the phone most of the morning. Alex kept one eye on his work and the other on the door to Tomas's office, waiting for an opportunity to retrieve the pen recorder.

He was mindlessly staring at his computer just before noon when Tomas emerged and headed for Roman's office. Just as Alex got to his feet, Greta came through the front door.

"Hey guys," she said to Alex and Lara, and then sat down at her desk. *Shit.* There was no way he could get into Tomas's office without her seeing.

"You gotta distract Greta so I can get into Tomas's

office," he whispered to Lara. Lara nodded. She went over to Greta and started talking to her, gradually moving to the far side of her desk to draw Greta's attention away from Tomas's door. *She's smart as well as beautiful,* Alex thought as he stood up. But before he could take a step, Tomas came out of Roman's office and went into his own.

Shit, Alex said to himself again. The next few hours passed slowly without Tomas leaving his office. At a little after one o'clock, a man with black hair brushed straight back and a bushy moustache walked into the travel agency. Tomas must have been expecting him because he came out of his office and motioned for the man to come inside.

"That's the guy from the restaurant," Alex whispered to Lara. "I bet he's brought the passport." He looked at Lara meaningfully. There was no need to elaborate. Tomas wasn't going to hold on to the passport for long. He would give to the Snowman the first chance he got. And then it would be game over.

Things were heating up. And the clock was counting down.

At a quarter to four, Roman walked down the hallway to the washroom. Tomas was in his office. Greta had already left so the coast was clear. "I'm going to do it now," he said to Lara. He texted Stefan. *We're on.*

K, Stefan texted back.

Alex hurried to the rear of the office and went through the door that led to the stairs down to the basement.

Now, he texted Stefan.

He opened the door a crack. A moment later Stefan came into the office and sat down at Alex's desk. He was wearing the same clothes as Alex, blue jeans and a white shirt. When Roman came out of the washroom, Stefan pretended he was on a call so Roman wouldn't ask him to do anything. He put the phone down when Roman returned to his office. He picked it up again a couple of minutes later when Tomas came out to speak to Lara. Alex couldn't help smiling as he watched Stefan nodding his head vigorously at something the imaginary caller was saying.

At four o'clock Lara and Stefan left the travel agency. Stefan was going to his practice. Lara would wait at the café and follow Tomas when he left the office. When Stefan's practice ended, he'd take over from Lara so she could go to hers. The timing had worked out perfectly.

Alex went downstairs and into the storage room. He sat on the floor, his back against the wall. He wondered how long he'd have to wait before Roman and Tomas left so he could get on Tomas's computer.

He played Angry Birds for a while until he saw that his phone battery was getting low. He couldn't take a chance on it dying. For the next hour or so he stared at the walls, wishing he'd remembered to bring something to read. At five thirty, Stefan texted him to say that he'd taken over from Lara so she could go to her practice. About an hour later, he sent another text to tell him that Roman had left, and a half hour after that, a third text informed him that Tomas was finally gone as well.

Alex stood up. His legs were stiff. He went upstairs, entered Tomas's office, and tapped on the keyboard to wake up the computer. He took the list of fifty-six plastic surgeons out of his pocket and put it on the desk. The first name on the list was Ray Allen. Alex entered Allen in the computer search field. It came up in seven emails.

Bingo. Alex couldn't believe his luck. He clicked on the

first email. It was to Tomas's dentist, Jack Allen. He opened the second email. d.allen@hotmail.com was one of the recipients of a group email Tomas had received from a store in Park Royal. By the third email, from Ed Allen, Lina's math tutor, Alex realized he was in for a long night. He was still working on Ray Allen when Stefan sent a text telling him that Tomas had gone straight home.

At nine fifteen he was on number twenty-seven, not quite halfway through the list, and feeling totally burned out. He took a break and called Stefan. "What's happening?" he asked.

"He's watching TV with Maria and Lina," Stefan said. "Looks like I'm going to be here for a while."

"You and me both, brother."

They were wrong. Fifteen minutes and four names later, Stefan called to say that Tomas was on the move.

"All right," Alex said excitedly.

"Doesn't mean anything," Stefan said. "He could just be going shopping."

Or he could be giving the passport to the Snowman, Alex thought. "Be careful."

"I'll call you as soon as I know anything."

Ten minutes after that Stefan called back with the worst possible news. "I lost him," he said glumly.

"What happened?"

"I got pulled over at a police road check on King Edward. Bummer."

Bummer wasn't the word he'd have used, Alex thought. When your car won't start, that's a bummer. When you forget to do your homework and the teacher calls on you in class, that's a bummer. When one of your father's murderers is about to disappear forever, that's not a bummer, that's a freaking disaster, but now wasn't the time

127

to explain the nuances of the English language to his brother.

"I'll let you know when he's back home," Stefan said. He was going back to Tomas's house. There was nothing they could do except stick with the game plan and pray that Tomas was just going shopping.

Alex clicked on the next email. It was from Rob Pascht, the plumber, not Jack Pascht, the plastic surgeon.

He had moved on to the next name, Bob Pettit, when he heard the front door of the agency open and shut. He turned off the desk light, shut down Tomas's computer, and quickly hid behind the couch.

The overhead lights in the office came on. *Guess Tomas didn't go shopping*, Alex said to himself. His heart was pounding. He tried to calm himself with the thought that there was no reason for Tomas to look behind the couch—until he realized he'd left the list of plastic surgeons on the desk. His heart leapt into his mouth.

He heard footsteps moving toward the desk. *I'm screwed. Worse than screwed*, he thought, when he imagined what Tomas and his "heroes" would do when they got hold of him. An image of Lara crying at his funeral flashed through his head.

Tomas's cellphone rang. "Hello … I'm here. I'll be right out."

Alex heard Tomas walk out of the office. He hurried to the desk, retrieved the list, and vaulted back into his hiding place.

"Take a seat," Tomas said to his visitor when he came back in.

"Nice office," a man said, as he sat down on the couch Alex was hiding behind. The springs groaned.

For a moment Alex thought it was the Snowman, come

to pick up his passport. Then he realized it couldn't be him. If it was the Snowman, he and Tomas would be speaking in Berovian.

"Here's the rest of the money," Tomas said. "Fifteen thousand. In hundreds."

"Here's the passport," the man said. Alex was confused. He thought Tomas already had the passport. Then he realized the man with the bushy moustache mustn't have given the passport to Tomas when he came to the agency in the afternoon.

"It looks perfect," Tomas said a few moments later. Alex heard a desk drawer open and close. He wondered if Tomas had put the passport in the drawer. If he did, Alex would be able to find out the Snowman's new identity. Provided he didn't get discovered. Because if he did ... Alex preferred not to think what would happen then.

"Your friend's brother won't have any trouble getting into the country with that," the man on the couch said. *Getting into the country? The Snowman's already here. And what was this about his friend's brother?* Alex's confusion returned. But only momentarily. Tomas wouldn't want anybody to know who the passport was for, or what it was for. The invention of a friend's brother was his cover story.

"That's going to make a lot of people happy," Tomas said. "His entire family is here." *A good cover story.*

"Why couldn't he come here legally?"

"He has a criminal record," Tomas said. *A great cover story ... You got to hand it to him,* Alex said to himself with grudging admiration. *He's thought of everything.*

"How about a drink?" Tomas asked. "I have some excellent slivovitz."

"I won't say no."

A few seconds later Alex heard the clink of glasses.

"*Dos prosta,*" Tomas said.

"Cheers. This is nice," the man said. He leaned back and put his arms over the back of the couch. Alex could see the rear of his head. There were rolls of fat on the back of his neck. His head was shaven. It wasn't the man Tomas met at the restaurant but Alex had a sneaking suspicion he knew who it was. And if he was right about that, then he was wrong about everything else.

"It's from Berovia."

"I've never been there. I hear it's beautiful."

"It is. You should take one of our tours," Tomas said.

"I might just do that. Okay, I gotta boogie."

Alex watched as a hat appeared on top of the bald head. One of those old-time hats, the kind you'd see in a black-and-white movie. The couch groaned again as the man stood up. The man groaned too, with the effort.

"Pleasure doing business with you," the man said.

The two men walked out of the office. Alex stayed behind the couch for a few minutes after the front door closed to make sure Tomas wasn't returning. Then he went to Tomas's desk and opened the drawer. A Canadian passport stared up at him. He flipped it open and studied the photograph of a young man with fierce black eyes and a bushy moustache. His name was Goran Berdich and he looked remarkably like the man Tomas met in the restaurant. In fact, he looked like he could be his brother.

Hey doofus, the Voice said, *you're just a kid. You're not going to catch the Stork and Snowman. Get it?*

Got it.

CHAPTER TWENTY-THREE

A week later things had more or less returned to normal.

When it came to the hunt for the Stork and the Snowman, Alex was back to where he'd been before he, Lara, and Stefan went off on their wild goose chase: haunted by his father's gruesome death, angry that his murderers had apparently vanished into thin air, and despairing that they would ever be brought to justice.

But Alex's mind was on happier thoughts when he came upstairs after breakfast. The Cougars had continued their stellar play, with three more wins since the victory over West Van ten days earlier, including a 5–1 shellacking of the fourth-place Abbotsford Miners the previous afternoon. The game was much closer than the score indicated but Alex had been in the zone, where it felt as if the game was being played in slow motion and the puck looked as big as a beach ball.

He put in a couple of hours' work on his English essay and then knocked on the door to Stefan's room. His brother was lying on his bed, a forlorn look on his face. He had played his worst game of the season the night before, letting in three goals he should have stopped in a 6–2 loss to Hollyburn. Alex had gone to the game and couldn't believe how poorly his brother had played.

"We have to get going," Alex said. Lara had made it to the title fight at the provincial muay Thai tournament and he and Stefan were going to the match.

"Okay," Stefan said without moving.

"It's only one game, dude," Alex said, trying to cheer up his brother. "Even the Wall has a bad game once in a while," he added, using Stefan's nickname for Lou Roberts. He called Lou "the Wall" because *lu* meant "wall" in Berovian.

"That's not the problem," Stefan said. "This is." He got up and went to his desk and handed Alex a couple of sheets of paper that were stapled together. It was his chemistry test from the week before. Forty-four percent was marked in red at the top.

"Holy shit," Alex said. He remembered Stefan saying the day before the test that he had everything under control.

"Yeah. At least I'm improving," Stefan said with a weak smile. "I got 42 percent on the first test."

"You said you got 78."

"I didn't want Mom and Dad to worry about me."

"Did you lie about your other courses, too?"

"No. I'm only having trouble with chemistry. I don't know what to do. If I don't pass ..." He didn't have to finish the sentence. They both knew what that would mean. Stefan wanted a scholarship to a U.S. college as much as Alex did, but if he didn't pass chemistry, he would have to go to summer school and by then all the scholarships would have been handed out. "I went to the teacher for help but he made me even more confused."

"Garnett's useless. I can help you."

"Really?"

"Sure. I'm doing well in chemistry."

"I don't have much time. The final exam's in a month," Stefan said.

"We can start tonight after your game."

"Thanks, man. I really appreciate it." Alex knew his brother's gratitude was sincere, but he could tell from the weak smile that he was by no means convinced his problems were over.

Lara was waiting outside Fraserview Hall when Alex and Stefan arrived.

"How are you feeling?" Alex asked.

"Nervous," she said. She was going up against her old nemesis, Tonya Livingstone, who had defeated her the year before.

"You'll be fine," he said. She looked past him, scanning the horizon. Alex knew she was looking for Jason. *I bet the prick doesn't show*, he said to himself.

"I'd better get inside and warm up," Lara said.

"Good luck."

"Thanks."

Alex and Stefan went to the Tims at the corner to get something to eat. When they got back to the arena, Lara's fight was about to start. She stood in one corner, dancing on her feet to stay loose, her black hair tied in a neat ponytail, a grim no-nonsense look on her face. Tonya stood in the other corner. She was shorter and more powerfully built than Lara.

The two girls stared each other down as the announcer introduced them. "This is the title match in the Junior Girls K One Lightweight class. In the blue corner, wearing red trunks, from Vancouver, weighing one hundred twenty-one pounds, Lara Wellington."

Alex and Stefan cheered, along with Lara's teammates and friends.

"In the red corner," the PA announcer continued,

"wearing white trunks, from Chilliwack, weighing one hundred twenty-five pounds, Tonya Livingston."

Tonya's supporters cheered and clapped just as enthusiastically.

"She looks mean," Stefan said. "I hope Lara doesn't get hurt."

"Don't worry about Lara," Alex said. "She can take care of herself."

Lara slipped her mouth guard into her mouth. As she walked into the middle of the ring to receive the referee's instructions, Jason walked into the gym. He made eye contact with Lara and held up his fist in a gesture of support. A big smile momentarily flashed across Lara's face before she put her game face back on. Jason took a seat in the stands a few rows in front of Alex, beside a cute redhead who was there with a friend.

Both fighters started out cautiously, sizing each other up. The first round ended with each fighter landing a few good blows, but none that did any damage. Alex noticed that Jason was paying more attention to the redhead than to the fight.

The second round was much like the first. Lara was quicker than Tonya but she wasn't using her speed to her advantage. Her coach was urging her to attack and with a minute left in the round, she did just that, landing a flurry of kicks and punches that had her opponent reeling and brought Alex and Stefan to their feet. Jason was still engrossed in conversation with the redhead.

Tonya grabbed hold of Lara, hanging on to give herself a chance to recover. The referee stepped in to separate them. As Lara stepped back, Tonya landed a punch flush on her face. She immediately held her hands up, as if to say it was an accident, but it was no accident. The referee gave her a warning and looked at Lara to make sure she was okay. She nodded, wiping her lip with a glove. It had already started to swell. A fierce look crossed her face.

"It's over," Alex said.

"She's not hurt that bad," Stefan said.

"That's not what I meant," Alex said. He'd seen that look on Lara's face before.

The referee signaled for the two girls to start fighting again. Tonya rushed in, thinking she had Lara in trouble. Lara stepped aside and snapped a hard punch to Tonya's stomach, causing her to drop her guard for just a moment, giving Lara enough time to launch a vicious kick to the side of Tonya's head that sent the girl from Chilliwack to the canvas. She landed with a thud that left no doubt that she was down for the count.

Ten seconds later Lara was the provincial champion.

Alex and Stefan jumped to their feet, cheering madly. As they walked down the aisle. Jason joined them. "Hey, Alex," he said. "What a great fight."

"Too bad you missed it," Alex said.

Jason ignored him. "You must be Alex's brother," he said to Stefan.

"You think?" Alex said.

Jason ignored that, too. "I'm Jason."

"Stefan." They shook hands.

Alex waited for him to say something stupid about how much they looked alike but Jason surprised him. "Lara told me how you guys found each other," he said, shaking his head in wonder. "Awesome."

"It was heavy," Stefan said.

Lara was pressing an ice pack against her lip. She smiled, and waved at them with the hand that held the ice pack, revealing a badly swollen lip.

"Won't be kissing that for a while," Jason whispered.

That's the jerk we know and love, Alex said to himself.

"You were great, babe," Jason said to Lara, giving her a hug. He looked over her head, his eyes tracking the redhead as she and her friend left the gym. Lara put the ice pack back on her lip. "That must really hurt," Jason said.

"It's nothing," Lara said.

"You smoked that girl," Alex said.

"Yeah. You were incredible," added Stefan.

"Awesome," Jason added.

"Thanks," Lara said, beaming at Jason. *Open your eyes,* Alex wanted to yell.

"When are the nationals?" Alex asked. Lara's victory meant that she would be competing at the national championships.

"Not until March. I've got five months to get ready and I'll need all of them."

"We'd better get going," Jason said. "Eddie said to come by any time after three."

Lara touched her lip. "This is going to gross everybody out."

"You'll still be the best-looking girl at the party," Jason said. Lara beamed again. *How can she not see that he's a phony?*

"You don't like him, do you?" Stefan said after Jason and Lara walked away.

"Not much," Alex said. Jason said something that made Lara laugh. She put her arm around his shoulder.

"You sure you're not jealous?"

"No, man. I already told you, we're just friends. I don't think he cares about her."

"That must be it," Stefan said.

CHAPTER TWENTY-FOUR

"I'll meet you in the library after school," Alex said to Stefan the next morning as they walked into school. The chemistry tutoring campaign was about to begin in earnest. They had a month to prepare for the final exam, but judging by the way things had gone the night before, Alex wasn't sure that would do the trick.

"Okay," Stefan said dully.

"It's going to be okay, man," Alex said with a confidence he didn't feel.

"For sure," Stefan said without conviction, and then trudged off to class.

Lara was at her locker. "How's the lip?" Alex asked.

"So-so." Lara lisped on account of her swollen lip. Tho-tho.

"It lookth thore," Alex said. "Exthtweemly thore. I hope it feelth better thoon."

"You're hilariouth. Who writeth your material?" Lara lisped.

Alex laughed. "How was the party?" he asked.

"Fine," she said, in a tone of voice that made Alex think it hadn't been all that fine. *Trouble in paradise?* he wondered, but the look on Lara's face suggested that the thought would be best kept to himself.

"Coach wants to see you," Neil Daniels said when Alex walked into the locker room before the Cougars game against the Langley Lions.

"I'm going to start Earl tonight," Hampton said when Alex came into his office. "It's got nothing to do with the way you're playing. You've been solid as a rock. But Earl needs to get some game experience under his belt."

"No problem," Alex said. He wasn't exactly happy about it—he'd come to the arena to play, not sit on the bench—but he knew it was the right move for the coach to make. If Alex got injured—*or if you screw up*, the Voice pointed out, just in case Alex wasn't aware of the possibility—Bales would have to step in and the coach needed to make sure he would be ready. Earl had played well in practice all year, but no matter how competitive a practice was, it could never measure up to the pressure of a real game.

"How are you feeling?" Alex asked Bales when he went back into the locker room.

"Nervous," Earl admitted.

"Just do the things we worked on in practice and you'll be fine," Alex said reassuringly. "Play the angles, hold your ground, and force the shooter to make the first move."

Bales left his nervousness in the locker room. Langley tested him right from the opening face-off, but the big rookie handled everything the Lions threw at him. By the time Richmond walked off the ice with a 3–1 victory, everybody knew that he would be ready if the team had to call on him.

Alex was reminded of a line from one of Johnny Chin's movies, where he played a martial arts master training a young novice. "Nothing pleases a teacher more than when his student surpasses him." *Yeah, right*, Alex thought. He and Johnny would have to agree to disagree about that one.

"Great game," Alex said to Bales in the locker room after the game. He wasn't prepared to say that the student had surpassed the teacher, but he knew it was close. Damn close.

"Thanks to you," Bales said graciously. Alex nodded. He and Earl exchanged a look. They both knew that Bales's performance, good as it was, didn't change anything. As well as he had played, they both knew that Alex was the starting goaltender. *Until you mess up*, the Voice reminded him.

Alex had no intention of messing up. If he did, he had a sneaking suspicion that he might never get his starting job back. It reminded him of a story in a book about sports heroes that Anna had given him a couple of years earlier for his birthday. In the story, an old-time baseball player named Wally Pipp, the starting first baseman for the New York Yankees, went into a slump. The coach replaced him with a player named Lou Gehrig. Gehrig played 2130 straight games, a record that lasted for more than fifty years, and Wally Pipp never got back into the starting lineup. Alex had no desire to play Wally Pipp to Earl Bales's Lou Gehrig.

The locker room suddenly went silent as Mike Leonard snuck up behind Neil Daniels who was kneeling on the floor, stuffing the game jerseys into a laundry bag. Mike tapped Neil on the shoulder. When Neil turned around, Leonard farted in his face.

Neil instinctively recoiled. He fell over the laundry bag and onto the floor. He lay there for a moment, his glasses hanging crookedly on his nose, a comical look on his face. Everybody broke out into laughter. Alex laughed in spite of himself.

"You're an asshole, Leonard," Neil said.

Leonard turned his butt toward him and farted again. More laughter. This time Alex didn't join in.

"Do you know when we're going to find out about the Hollyburn tournament?" Alex asked Kenny Nelson as they headed to the front door of the arena after changing into their street clothes.

The Hollyburn Invitational was the most prestigious tournament of the season. Eight of the top teams in the province would be there. And so would scouts from every major college in the States and every junior hockey team in Western Canada.

"Not for another month but we'll get an invite for sure."

"Unless we fall apart," Alex said.

"That's not going to happen," Kenny said confidently.

"I hope you're right," Alex said. "Shit. I left my knapsack in the locker room. I'll see you later."

"Later."

Everybody had left by the time Alex returned to the locker room. His knapsack was on the floor, right where he left it. He picked it up and was about to leave when he heard a sound coming from the washroom. He peeked inside. Neil Daniels was sitting on the floor in the corner. He was crying. He must have known somebody was there but he didn't look up. Alex hesitated for a second, unsure whether to say something, before turning and walking away.

Alex thought about Neil all the way home. It wasn't just the farting incident that had triggered Neil's tears. It was the culmination of two years of being harassed and bullied by

Mike Leonard. Alex realized that he'd known how Neil felt all along but he'd deluded himself into thinking that Neil didn't really mind so that he wouldn't feel bad about doing nothing. Well, he couldn't delude himself any longer, not after what he'd just seen.

But what should he do about? What *could* he do about it? Adults were always saying that bullies are cowards, that if you stand up to a bully he'll back down, but everybody knew that was a pile of crap. Alex knew exactly what would happen if he said anything. *What are you going to do about it, Petrovic?* Mike Leonard would say with a smirk on his face. And then what would he do? He would have to put up or shut up. Putting up meant being willing to fight Leonard, and if he did that, he didn't stand a chance. Leonard could beat the piss out of Alex with one arm tied behind his back.

That was the truth, no matter what the adults tried to tell you, but knowing that didn't make Alex feel any better about doing nothing while Mike Leonard terrorized poor Neil Daniels.

CHAPTER TWENTY-FIVE

The Cougars won five more games in the three weeks following their victory over Langley, raising their record to an unblemished 12–0, but Alex was feeling anxious about that night's game against Hollyburn. The Huskies had also been on a roll and were in second place, only two games behind Richmond. West Van had won three of its last four and was in third place, two more games back. The early season prediction that the three teams would be vying for the championship was right on the money.

Alex hoped his team would be ready for the game. The Cougars hadn't faced a strong opponent for a while and he was concerned that the team had crossed the fine line between confidence and overconfidence. They seemed to think that all they had to do to win was show up. Coach Hampton had warned them that sooner or later their attitude would catch up to them and Alex had a sinking feeling that tonight might be the night.

An email alert from the War Crimes Tribunal Twitter feed interrupted his thoughts. It was the first one he'd received in weeks and he opened it with a sense of excitement that evaporated the moment he read it. The authorities had upped the reward to $500,000, more proof, if more proof was needed, that they didn't have the faintest idea where the Stork or the Snowman were.

He could hear Anna and Stefan talking in the kitchen

when he went downstairs.

"Don't tell me nothing's wrong," Anna was saying. "You've been moping around the house for the past few weeks like there's a black cloud over your head."

"I'm just upset with the way I'm playing," Stefan said.

Alex knew that hockey wasn't the real reason his brother was down in the dumps, although his play of late was a far cry from the way he was capable of playing. Chemistry, not hockey, was the source of Stefan's woes. He and Alex had been working hard, putting in an hour or two every day, but they'd had to start from square one and there was a lot of ground to cover. Even though Stefan had made a lot of progress, he'd dug himself a big hole by failing the first two tests. Alex was confident his brother would pass the exam but it was worth only a third of his final mark and he needed to get 66 percent to raise his overall mark up to a passing grade. And with only one week to go, Alex wasn't sure his brother would make it.

Anna turned to Alex as he walked into the kitchen. Stefan gave him a warning look. Something was up.

"I just spoke to the insurance company," Anna said in the extra quiet, extra calm voice she used when she was extra angry, "to find out why our premiums went up by five hundred dollars. Care to guess what they told me?"

"Not really," Alex said. *Five hundred dollars!*

"Running a light and illegally passing another vehicle. On the same day. Would you mind explaining how this happened?" Alex looked at Stefan. "Don't look at your brother. He can't help you."

Alex shrugged. There was no point trying to explain. If he told her what really happened, he'd just get in more trouble.

"Were you drinking?" she asked accusingly.

"No." She looked at him searchingly and then nodded, satisfied he was telling the truth.

"I'm sorry, Mom," he said. "I'll pay for the increase in the insurance." Together with the road fines, the damage was close to eight hundred dollars. He could forget about getting the Vespa in time for summer.

"You're darn right you will," she said. "We'll leave in five minutes," she said to Stefan. He nodded. She turned to Alex. "Are you coming with us?"

"I'll take the bus," Alex said. Normally he'd jump at the chance for a lift to school even though he had a spare first period, but he'd rather not give Anna another opportunity to get on his case.

Alex played video games on his computer until it was time to leave. When he went into the washroom, he noticed a faint shadow of a beard on his face and decided to shave.

He had started shaving a year ago. At first he only had to shave once a week, but recently he'd noticed he had to shave more often. His beard was still kind of patchy so the unshaven look that a lot of the guys sported didn't suit him. It just made him look scruffy.

He softened his beard with hot water before lathering his face with shaving cream. It occurred to him that most boys were taught how to shave by their fathers; he'd learned from a YouTube video. He took his razor and started shaving, making sure to shave in the direction his hair grew just like they showed in the video.

The blade scraped roughly against his face. He dug into his shaving kit for a new blade but he was fresh out. He took Stefan's shaving kit out of the cabinet. As he was rummaging around for a blade, he spotted a box of condoms. He opened the box. There were only two left from the twelve that came in the box. It confirmed what he already knew. Stefan and Emma were having sex.

He put a fresh blade in his razor and stared at himself in the mirror. *Are you ever going to get laid?*

"Shit," he said aloud a moment later. A thin line of blood was trickling down his cheek. The video had warned him to pay attention. He stuck a piece of Kleenex on the cut and finished shaving. This time he kept his eyes on the mirror, but his thoughts kept straying.

Alex opened his locker and put the books he'd need for the day in his knapsack. Lara caught up to him as he was walking to English class. She looked different. It took Alex a few seconds to figure out what had changed.

"You cut your hair," he said. "It looks nice." She looked better than nice. She looked fantastic.

Lara beamed. "Thanks. I like your new look, too."

"What do you mean?" he asked.

"You've got a piece of Kleenex on your face."

He couldn't believe he'd left the house like that. "Cut myself shaving," he said. He felt a slight tug as he pulled the tissue away from the cut. *That was dumb.* They warned him not to do that on the video.

"Now you're bleeding," Lara said, shaking her head at his stupidity. She took a Kleenex from her bag and dabbed Alex's cheek. He felt his body tingle as she brushed up against him. He had an overpowering urge to kiss her. Lara handed him the tissue. "Just pat it," she said. "Don't leave it on, or the same thing will happen again."

Her phone rang. She checked the display. "Talk to you later?" she said to Alex in a tone of voice that made it clear she wanted to take the call in private. He nodded and walked away. "Hey, Jason," she said into the phone, her voice rising with excitement. If there had been any trouble between her and Jason, they'd clearly worked things out. When he saw the smile on her face Alex felt a pang of … a pang of what? *And what was that all about?* he asked himself, referring to his desire to kiss her. But he knew the answer to both questions. He just didn't know what to do about it.

CHAPTER TWENTY-SIX

Alex's fear that the team wasn't ready for Hollyburn was well founded. The Cougars came out flat and if Alex hadn't been as sharp as he had been, they would have been out of the game by the end of the first period. As it was, with five minutes left in the game, they were down 3–1 and their prospects looked bleak. Then Mike Leonard banged home a rebound and suddenly the Cougars were within a goal of tying the game. But less than a half-minute later, Doug Harvey was sent to the penalty box for hooking.

Alex pounded his stick against his pads, his eyes focused on the puck as if it were the only object in the universe. If Richmond gave up a goal on the power play, it was game over.

For the next two minutes the Huskies swarmed around the Richmond goal, but Alex managed to hold them off. With thirty seconds left in the power play, Bill Kelly intercepted a pass and hit Mike Leonard at the blue line, catching the Hollyburn defensemen out of position. Leonard put on a burst of speed, broke in on the Hollyburn goal, and fired a shot past the Huskies' goalie to even the score. His Richmond teammates erupted in cheers.

With a minute left in the game, and the teams at full strength, Leonard converted a nifty pass from Kenny Nelson to give the Cougars a 4–3 victory.

Leonard's three goals in a row gave him a rare natural hat trick, and one old-school fan threw his hat onto the ice to celebrate it. Alex had seen it done at NHL games but this was the first time it had ever happened in a game he played in. Stevie Ryan picked up the hat and gave it to Leonard. He put it on and skated off the ice as the Cougars fans cheered.

Leonard's heroics had saved the day and the big forward was the man of the hour in the locker room after the game. Alex collapsed onto the bench in front of his locker and watched the celebration. He was tired but it was a good kind of tired. He took off his jersey. It was drenched with sweat.

"I'll take that," Neil Daniels said.

Alex handed the shirt to him. "Thanks, Neil." Alex hadn't called him Pie ever since the day he saw him crying in the washroom.

"You're welcome," Neil said. He had never said anything about it but Alex knew he appreciated the gesture. Alex watched as Neil approached Mike Leonard. Leonard handed Neil his shirt without a comment. He had pretty much ignored Neil ever since the farting incident. Alex was beginning to think that Leonard realized he'd crossed the line. At least that's what he was hoping. He'd made a promise to himself that he would do something the next time Leonard bullied Neil, but it was okay with him if he was never called upon to honor it.

"Listen up," Coach Hampton said as he walked into the locker room. The noise died down. "That was a lucky win. We played like crap. We got away with it tonight but I hope you all got the wake-up call. We need to get back to what got us here. Everybody giving 100 percent effort, 100 percent of the time. Agreed?" Hampton looked around the room. Everybody nodded. They knew he was right. "Okay, then," he said. "One other thing. Don't make any plans for the holidays because we've been invited to play in the Hollyburn Invitational."

Everybody cheered.

Alex felt excited even though the tournament was a month away. Bill Henry's words reverberated in his head. *You got some serious game.* He looked at the University of Minnesota hockey sweater hanging in his locker. Maybe, just maybe, he'd be wearing the real thing next year.

"Any other teams from our league get invited, aside from Hollyburn?" Paul Arizin called out. As the host team, Hollyburn got an automatic invite.

"Just West Van," Coach Hampton said. *Just West Van.* The same scouts Alex was hoping to impress would also be taking a look at Stefan and none of them were going to recruit two goalies. *No, they're not,* the Voice agreed. Alex felt a twinge of sibling rivalry but it didn't last long. If Stefan played in the tournament the way he'd been playing the past few weeks, Alex knew he didn't have a thing to worry about. And if Stefan didn't pass chemistry it wouldn't matter how well he played. Not that he wished either of these misfortunes on his brother. *Of course not,* said the Voice.

"Practice tomorrow at six," Hampton said before disappearing into his office.

The announcement that the team had been invited to the Hollyburn tournament set off another round of celebration. Mike Leonard strutted through the locker room, wearing his hat and waving his jockstrap over his head. He walked up behind Neil Daniels, who was cutting up oranges to give out to the players.

"Hey, Pie. You get a hat, too," he shouted as he put his

jockstrap over Neil's head and then pinned his arms to his side so he couldn't take it off.

"Get away from me," Neil yelled. Leonard laughed and released him. Neil tore the jockstrap off and threw it on the floor. He looked close to tears.

"Gonna squirt a few, Pie?" Leonard mocked. He coughed the word *faggot*. As usual, half the team laughed and the other half stared at their skates.

Oh shit, Alex thought. *Time to put up or shut up.* He got to his feet. "Cut it out, Mike. Stop being such a prick."

Leonard drew himself up to his full six feet three inches and looked down at Alex. "What did you say?"

"Leave Neil alone," Alex said. His voice was firm even though his insides were quaking.

"Me and Pie are just having some fun."

"His name's Neil," Alex said.

"Pie knows I'm just joking around, don't you, Pie?" Leonard put Neil in a headlock, pulling his head toward his bare sweaty chest. Neil squirmed but he couldn't get free.

"Let him go," Alex said.

"Make me." Leonard glared at Alex.

"C'mon you guys, relax," Don Herron said.

"Shut your face," Leonard yelled at him. He approached Alex, backing him up against the wall. "What are you going to do about it, Petrovic?" Alex pushed him away. Hard. Leonard rushed at him and punched him in the jaw. Before he could hit him again, a few of the other guys grabbed him and held him back.

Coach Hampton burst into the room. "What's going on here?" he demanded. He looked at Alex and then at Leonard. It was pretty clear what was going on.

"Nothing, Coach," Alex said. Hampton looked at Leonard.

"We were just fooling around, Coach," Leonard said. Hampton turned to Alex.

"Just fooling around," Alex echoed. He could feel his jaw swelling up.

Hampton nodded but Alex knew he wasn't buying it. "You guys get dressed and go on home," he said and then stomped out of the room.

"This isn't over, Petrovic," Leonard said.

"Don't be a jerk, Mike," Doug Harvey said.

"Screw you," Leonard said.

"Stop being such a moron," Bill Kelly said.

"Faggot," Leonard said, using his fake cough, trying to defuse the situation. This time nobody laughed. He looked around the room for some support but even Stevie Ryan turned away.

"You guys are a bunch of babies," Leonard said without conviction. He sat down and finished dressing. The normal locker room chatter slowly resumed.

"Hey, Neil," Doug Harvey called out. "Are there any more oranges?"

"I'll take one too, Neil."

By the time Alex got home, his jaw was throbbing. He put some more ice on it and took a couple of aspirin but it still hurt like hell.

He'd never felt better in his entire life.

CHAPTER TWENTY-SEVEN

Alex didn't know what he'd done to piss Lara off but he must have done something because there she was, in the middle of the ring, staring at him with the determined look on her face that generally spelled trouble for anyone unlucky enough to be in there with her.

"You asked for it, Petrovic," she said, as she slowly advanced toward him. The next thing he knew, Lara had him pinned on the canvas. "You asked for it," she said again. But instead of raining blows on him, she lowered her face toward his. Their lips were about to meet when the bell rang, signaling the end of the round. It rang and rang.

It kept ringing until Alex realized his alarm was going off. He reached over, turned it off, and then lay back on his bed, thinking about the dream. You didn't have to be a shrink to figure it out, as Lara would have said. He wasn't exactly sure when his feelings toward her had changed, but there was no denying they had. Too bad he had no idea what to do about it, but at least he had a couple of weeks to figure it out. Today was the last day of school before the winter holidays and Lara was going to Mexico with her parents.

Last day of school, Alex repeated to himself with a smile as he got out of bed and started doing his push-ups. The prospect of two weeks without classes must have energized him because for the first time ever he was able to do one hundred push-ups. He collapsed on the floor when he finished, completely spent but completely satisfied. He rested for a minute and did his sit-ups before heading to the washroom. Stefan was coming up the stairs.

"Last day of school, dude," Alex said.

"Yeah."

"You nervous?"

"What do you think?" Stefan snapped. "Sorry," he quickly added.

"That's okay," Alex said. Stefan had good reason to be on edge. The report cards were being handed out today. Stefan thought he'd done well on his chemistry exam, but he didn't know if he got the 66 percent he needed and it would be another six hours or so before he found out.

"You'll be fine," Alex predicted.

"We'll see," Stefan said with a shrug. "Mom wanted me to remind you that we're having dinner at Lombardo's. I'm picking her up here after I get Dad so I can get you, too, or we can meet at the restaurant." Boris was coming to Vancouver that afternoon and was going to spend the holidays with Stefan.

"I'll meet you here. It's great that your dad is going to be here for so long."

"It won't be so great if I flunked chem."

"You're the one who's always telling me to be positive."

"You're right … Nice win last night," Stefan said. Richmond had defeated Abbotsford 3–1, upping its record to a perfect sixteen and zero. "Are you guys ever going to lose a game?"

"Not planning on it."

The Cougars had come together off the ice as well as on it in the month since Alex's fight with Mike Leonard.

Leonard had stopped torturing Neil Daniels, and without that divisive element in the locker room the team's morale had skyrocketed. The entire team had hung out for an hour in the locker room after the game against Abbotsford, just chewing the fat. It was the kind of intangible that could translate to a championship.

Alex had played another good game, but he would have had a shutout if he hadn't misplayed a rebound that led to the Miners' lone goal. It was a harmless mistake—there were only a couple of minutes left in the game, and the Cougars were up 3–0 at the time—but it still rubbed him the wrong way.

Alex went back into his room and logged on to his computer. He didn't expect any news about the Stork and the Snowman and there wasn't any. It had been a month since the Berovian government had upped the reward to $500,000 and nobody had come forward. They could raise the reward to a million dollars, Alex thought, or even ten, and it wouldn't make any difference. He would just have to accept the fact that the men who murdered his father would never be brought to justice. Just thinking about it made his blood boil. He would never be able to accept it, he realized. He clicked on nhl.com to check last night's scores. All he could do was try not to think about it.

Alex walked out of English class at the end of the day feeling free as a bird. The hallway was full of students in full celebration mode. Alex took his books out of his knapsack and put them in his locker. *Won't be needing these for a while*, he thought. The only thing he kept was his report card. Anna would be pleased. And so was he. He was a little disappointed he hadn't done better than 72 in English, but his 78 average was the highest he'd ever had.

Stefan hurried up to him. The smile on his face said it all. "Made it by the skin of my teeth," he said, handing Alex his report card.

"Fifty-three percent," Alex said, looking at his brother's chemistry mark. "That means you got ..." He started to do the calculation.

"Seventy-three on the exam," Stefan said.

"Way to go, bro," Alex said. "You did it."

"Thanks to you," Stefan said, his face serious. "I owe you."

"Big time. And don't you forget it," he joked. He returned the report card to Stefan. He noticed that his brother's average was a respectable 73, well above the 67 he needed to qualify for a scholarship to a U.S. school.

"I mean it, man. If I hadn't passed ... oh man, I don't even want to think about what would have happened then." He sighed in relief, as if he'd had a near-death experience. "I got to go. I'm meeting Mom at the store to get the car and then I'm going to the airport to get Dad."

"Okay. I'll see you at the house."

Alex was locking up when Kenny Nelson came over. "Did you see the draw?" he asked.

"Yeah," Alex said. "Do you know anything about Kelowna?" The Hollyburn Invitational Tournament was starting the following week and Richmond was playing the Kelowna Rangers in the opening round.

"Just that they won their league championship last year, and they've only lost one game so far this year."

"They're going to be tough."

"They're all going to be tough ... We're going to need to bring our A game if we're going to win."

There was more than the tournament championship at stake, Alex thought. A lot of college scouts would be there.

If he was going to impress them, he'd need to bring his A game. He had a hunch Stefan would be bringing his.

When Alex got outside he saw Lara standing on the sidewalk. He was reminded of his dream. He wondered what she'd say if he told her about it.

"When do you leave for Mexico?" he asked.

"Tonight at seven. My mom's picking me up and then we're getting my dad and going straight to the airport." She didn't sound very excited about it. She didn't look very excited about it either. In fact, she looked downright sad.

"Are you okay?" he asked.

"Yes … No. Jason and I broke up."

"What happened?" Alex asked.

"I saw him with another girl."

"That doesn't mean anything. Maybe they were just friends." He wondered if it was the redhead from the gym.

"They were friendly, all right. He had his tongue halfway down her throat."

Told you so.

"Don't say 'I told you so,'" she warned.

"Wouldn't dream of it."

"And don't say you're sorry."

Alex nodded. Sorry was the exact opposite of how he felt. *Probably not a good idea to cheer*, he thought, but that's what he felt like doing. It took all his self-control not to tell her how he felt about her, but he knew it would be a mistake to spring it on her now.

"He's such a prick. I can't believe it took me this long to find out. I'm such a fool."

"He's the fool," Alex said hotly. "He doesn't know special you are."

Lara smiled. "What a nice thing to say."

"I mean it. He doesn't deserve you."

"You're sweet."

An awkward silence followed. It ended when Lara's mother drove up.

"See you later," Lara said as she got into the car. "Happy holidays."

"You, too."

Alex watched them drive away. *At least Jason is out of the picture*, he said to himself. That solved one of his problems. The other problem was what Lara would say when he told her how he felt.

CHAPTER TWENTY-EIGHT

"I'm starving," Boris said after they were seated at Lombardo's.

"Didn't they feed you on the airplane?" Anna asked.

"They gave us a tray of something. I'm not prepared to say it was food. Air Maldania has a motto," Boris said. "We're not happy until you're not happy." It took Alex a few seconds to get the joke.

A fat man with long black hair and a goatee sat by himself in the corner. The pitcher of beer on the table was nearly empty. He looked vaguely familiar but Alex couldn't place him. The waitress arrived with a portable credit machine. The man punched a few buttons and handed it back to her. He poured the rest of the beer into his glass and downed it in a single gulp.

Stefan's phone buzzed with a text message. He smiled as he read it.

"Emma?" Anna asked. Stefan nodded and texted a reply.

"Who else?" Alex said. Stefan and Emma texted each other a hundred times a day.

"She can meet us for lunch tomorrow," Stefan said to Boris.

"Great," said Boris. "I'm looking forward to meeting her."

"She's lovely," Anna said.

By now Lara was on her way to Mexico, Alex thought. He had no idea what he was going to say to her when she got back. And he had no idea how she'd respond. The one thing he did know was that it would be impossible to go on pretending that nothing had changed.

Just then his cellphone beeped. It was a text—from Stefan. *Don't worry, she's into you.*

Alex looked up. His brother winked at him. "I always knew it was just a matter of time before you two got together," he'd said earlier, when Alex told him that Lara and Jason had broken up. "You've got a vivid imagination," Alex had answered.

The fat man with the goatee got to his feet and walked toward the front door. He was unsteady on his feet. *Where have I seen him before?* Alex asked himself.

"Karl," Boris called out as the man walked by their table. The man stopped and looked at Boris blankly for a few seconds until he recognized him.

"Boris," he said, breaking into a smile. *"Mato le ti?"* How *are you?*

Boris stood up and they shook hands. "This is Karl Chillich," he said, introducing him to Anna, Stefan, and Alex. Alex noticed that Karl had one brown eye and one green eye—just like Lou Roberts—and realized he'd seen him at the airport after the first tour to Berovia and Maldania.

"This is Anna, Alex and Stefan," Boris said, identifying them only by name. It would be way too complicated to identify them by relationship. *This is my son, Stefan; his mother, Anna; and her son, Alex.* It looked like Karl was having enough trouble as it was.

"Karl was on the first tour," Boris said.

"Best tour ever," Karl said, slurring the words.

"Even if we did get a little more excitement than we bargained for on the way home," Boris said with a laugh.

Karl gave Boris a puzzled look.

"The bomb threat at the airport," Boris explained.

A confused look momentarily crossed Karl's face. "Of course," he said with a laugh to cover up his embarrassment. "I guess I've had a little too much to drink." *You think?* Alex said to himself. "Enjoy your meal," Karl said. "Merry Christmas," he added, before waddling away.

"I hope he's not driving," Anna said.

"I'll go check," said Boris. He followed Karl out of the restaurant. He came back a few minutes later. "I persuaded him to take a cab."

"He was actually planning to drive?" Anna asked in astonishment.

"He said he only lives a few minutes away."

Anna shook her head in disgust. "I hope you two know not to get in a car with someone who's been drinking," she said to Alex and Stefan.

They rolled their eyes at each other. "Yes, Mom," they both said with exaggerated patience.

"I don't care where you are. Call me and if I can't come get you, I'll pay for a taxi."

"Is the next tour fully booked?" Anna asked Boris after they placed their dessert orders. Boris and Roman's second tour was scheduled for mid-January.

"It is. And we have a bunch of people on the waiting list so we're going to do a third tour during March break. Roman and I thought you guys might want to come on it," Boris said to Alex and Stefan.

"That would be fantastic, wouldn't it, boys?" Anna

said.

"I'd love to go," Alex said, "but the provincial championships are being held the weekend after March break and we'll be practicing every day."

"I was just going to say the same thing," Stefan said.

"I guess you aren't aware that only one team from our league gets to go. The one that wins the league championship."

"I know that," Stefan said, "and you're going to have a great time in Berovia and Maldania."

"Lara's invited too," Boris said.

Maybe it won't be such a bad thing if West Van wins the championship, Alex couldn't help thinking. *Now who's the one with the vivid imagination?* he asked himself. Stefan winked at him again, as if he'd read his mind.

"Are you guys going to play against each other in the Hollyburn tournament?" Boris asked.

"Only if we both make the finals." Alex explained that Richmond and West Van were on opposite sides of the draw. Each team would have to win their first two games in order for them to meet in the final. "And that's not going to be easy," he added.

"Maybe not," Boris said, "but I have a feeling that's exactly what's going to happen."

The waitress came to the table. "We only have one slice of lemon meringue left," the waitress said.

"You can give it to my baby brother," Stefan said.

CHAPTER TWENTY-NINE

Boris's prediction turned out to be accurate. Richmond and West Van each won their first two games of the tournament, and the two teams were facing each other in the championship final.

The drive to Hollyburn's arena took place in silence. Anna and Boris were up front. Alex and Stefan sat in the back. Stefan was leaning back against the seat, his eyes closed, cool as a cucumber. With the chemistry monkey off his back, he'd brought his A game to the tournament, just as Alex had anticipated.

Alex had never been so nervous before a game in his entire life, and that was saying something. He had played well in the first two rounds, every bit as well as Stefan, but he'd need to keep it up in the championship final if he was going to impress the scouts. *It's only a game*, he told himself in a futile effort to calm his jittery nerves. It wasn't as if his life was at stake. *No*, the Voice agreed, *just your chance for a college scholarship.*

Anna dropped Alex and Stefan off near the entrance to the arena. "We'll see you after the game," Anna said.

"Good luck," Boris said.

Alex and Stefan walked into the arena together. Bill Henry was standing at the concession stand, talking to a man in a University of Washington jacket. The butterflies in Alex's stomach went into overdrive.

Richmond came out firing on all cylinders, taking the game to West Van from the get-go. The Cougars peppered Stefan with shots from all angles but they couldn't put the puck past him. If you didn't know better, you could have been excused for thinking it was Lou Roberts behind the white mask. *Did you see that?* the Voice marveled after Stefan dove across the crease to rob Bill Kelly of a certain goal. *Even Lou couldn't have made that save. The scouts must be drooling.* Alex's nerves tightened another notch with every miraculous save. He could feel his confidence sagging. He knew he couldn't possibly match his brother's performance.

The game was four minutes old before he faced his first shot. West Van's left-winger carried the puck over center ice and flicked a high lazy shot toward him before heading to the bench for a line change.

The shot was as easy as they come but it caught Alex napping. He stayed in his crease, realizing too late that he should have come out of the net to catch the puck while it was still in the air. It landed a few feet in front of him, took a crazy bounce, skipped past him, and before he could react, it was in the goal.

Alex stared at the puck in disbelief. He hadn't misplayed a shot like that since he was an Atom. *Biggest game of your life, and you let in a goal like that,* the Voice said in disgust as Alex angrily swept the puck out of the goal.

Alex took a sip of water, skated to the corner of the rink, and then got back in position. He remembered what his first coach had told him. "A good goalie needs a bad memory." It meant that you had to forget about a mistake as soon as you made it. If your mind stayed in the past, you couldn't be ready for the present.

Doug Harvey skated up to him. "Shake it off, big guy," he said. "We'll get it back."

But the Cougars couldn't get it back. And Alex couldn't shake it off.

Three minutes later he paid the price for his lack of focus, letting in another goal when he failed to hug the post on a routine shot from the wing.

Two minutes before the first period ended, Alex was slow to get to his feet after making a save, leading to another West Van goal that gave the Lightning a 3–0 lead at the first intermission.

Coach Hampton stopped Alex on his way to the locker room. "It's not your day, Alex. I'm going to put Earl in," he said bluntly.

The rest of the game passed in a blur. Alex sat on the bench, numb, barely registering the action on the ice. He'd never been pulled from a game before, let alone a game that meant this much. He felt humiliated, as if he were sitting there naked with everybody in the arena staring at him. He wished the ground would open up and swallow him live.

Earl Bales played well, giving up only one goal in the last two periods, but getting the puck past Stefan was a puzzle Richmond couldn't solve. West Van ended up winning by a score of 4–0.

Alex stood by the boards with his teammates as the championship trophy was presented to West Van and the tournament all-stars were announced. He applauded when Stefan received the tournament most valuable player award, but inside he felt the jealousy rise up like a tidal wave. He wished the clock could be turned back to the start of the game so he could have another chance. But he'd had his chance. *And you blew it, dude*, the Voice said. *You choked in the biggest game of your life.*

His teammates went out of their way to reassure him in the locker room.

"Everybody has a bad game, big guy."

"This doesn't count in the league standings. We're still in first place."

"No worries, dude. We'll get them next time, when it counts."

The kind words didn't make him feel any better.

At least it can't get any worse, he told himself when he finally managed to drag himself out of the locker room. Then he looked across the hallway … and saw Stefan deep in conversation with Bill Henry.

CHAPTER THIRTY

Coach Hampton called Alex into his office before practice two days after the loss to West Van.

"How are you doing?" he asked. Alex shrugged, averting the coach's gaze. He knew what was coming. It had kept him awake all night. He was about to lose his starting position. Hampton would be decent about it, but no amount of sugarcoating was going to make this pill any easier to swallow.

"You had a bad game," the coach said. "There's no getting away from it." He waited until Alex looked at him. "I don't know who was wearing your uniform, but it wasn't the guy who's led this team all year, the guy I'm counting on to do the job against Hollyburn on Thursday." Alex looked at the coach in surprise. "You're still my starting goalie, son. Even Lou Roberts has a bad game once in a while. And he always bounces back with a great game." *Too bad you're not Lou Roberts*, the Voice said.

They talked for a while after that but everything the coach said boiled down to the same thing Alex's first coach told him: "A good goalie needs a bad memory."

It was good advice, but no matter how hard he tried, Alex couldn't follow it. His memory was just too damn good. The next two weeks were the most miserable two weeks of his life.

Three days after Coach Hampton's pep talk, Alex stumbled through a subpar performance against Hollyburn, letting in three goals he should have stopped in a 4–3 loss. It was the team's first defeat in the regular season.

He followed that up the next week with a horrendous outing against Aldershot. Only a last-minute goal by Kenny Nelson allowed Richmond to escape with a 5–5 tie and avoid a second consecutive loss.

Then, two days after that, the bottom fell out with an abysmal performance in a 4–2 loss to the cellar-dwelling Chilliwack Condors.

Alex was playing as if he'd never strapped on a pair of pads, so he wasn't surprised when Hampton called him into his office before the game against West Van and told him that Earl Bales was getting the starting nod.

"I don't like doing this, Alex, but I don't have a choice," the coach said sympathetically. Alex nodded in understanding. If he was a position player, the coach might have been willing to stick with him. But when a goalie played badly, it could affect the rest of the team and that's exactly what had happened. His teammates had lost confidence in him. In the past they knew they could count on Alex to bail them out if they made a mistake. Now they were playing tentatively, afraid that a mistake would lead to an opponent's goal.

"I know you're disappointed," Hampton continued. Alex nodded again but in fact he was relieved. He'd been dreading the rematch against his brother all day. He would never have imagined that one day he would prefer to sit on the bench rather than play, but that day had come. "I don't know how Earl's going to handle the pressure," the coach continued, "so you need to keep your head in the game and be ready if I call on you." Alex nodded again, but he hoped it wouldn't come to that. *Amen*, the Voice said.

Alex's wish was granted. Earl Bales was solid from the opening face-off. Richmond started out playing cautious hockey, but the rookie made three great saves in the early going that restored the Cougars' confidence. They went on the offensive and didn't let up for the entire game.

Stefan was his usual magnificent self, but his West Van teammates were completely outplayed by a rejuvenated Richmond squad who cruised to a convincing 3–1 victory.

The entire team piled out onto the ice after the game to congratulate Earl and the celebration continued in the locker room. The gloom that had descended on the team since the Hollyburn tournament flowed out of the room; the belief that they were a championship-caliber team flooded back in.

"Great game, Earl," Alex said.

"Thanks," Earl said. He looked Alex in the eye to let him know that he understood how Alex was feeling. Alex nodded but he knew Earl didn't have a clue how he felt. Earl thought that he was disappointed about losing his starting position and that he had been hoping Earl would play poorly so that Hampton would put him back between the pipes. That's how most people in his position would feel. But that wasn't the situation. To the contrary. Alex had been praying that Earl would play well so that he could stay on the bench where he would be safe, where he wouldn't have to suffer another public humiliation.

He'd lost his mojo and he didn't know if he was ever going to get it back.

Want me to wait for you? Stefan texted as Alex watched his teammates celebrate the victory.

Go ahead. I'll see you at home, Alex texted back.

You okay?

I'm good.

Lara was waiting in the corridor when Alex finally emerged from the locker room.

"How are you doing?" she asked sympathetically. Alex shrugged. "Do you want to get a coffee?"

"I can't," he lied. "I have too much homework to do."

"It's Friday night," Lara pointed out. "You have all weekend to do your homework."

"I'm way behind," he said. The words were out of his mouth before he realized how lame they were. School had only started two weeks ago. He couldn't possibly be that far behind. "I'll see you at work tomorrow."

"Suit yourself," she said, not bothering to call him on his obvious lie, or to hide the fact that she was pissed off. Lara had been trying to get him to open up ever since she got back from Mexico, but he had shut her out. He couldn't bear to talk about what happened. And as to his resolution to tell her how he felt about her, there was no way he was up to that. He wasn't sure he had any feelings for her. Or for anybody else. He was too busy feeling sorry for himself.

He watched Lara as she walked away. He wished she'd turn around and come back, but he knew she wouldn't. And he didn't have it in him to go after her.

Alex lay in bed that night, unable to fall asleep. He'd been having the best season of his career. *How could things have fallen apart so quickly?* he asked himself. But he knew the reason: a case of sibling rivalry that turned into a train wreck. He had never come to terms with the fact that Stefan was a better goalie than he was. It was like a sore he kept scratching but never allowed to heal. His brother's heroics at the start of the tournament final, with all those scouts in attendance, tore off the scab and while Alex was watching it bleed, he let in that ridiculous first goal. From then on it was game over.

He got out of bed and started playing his hockey video game to get his mind off his troubles. He played for a couple of hours until he could barely keep his eyes open. As he logged off, he noticed that he'd received a Twitter alert from the War Crimes Tribunal. He clicked on the link. One glance at the headline and his eyes were wide open.

ZARKOV ESCAPES: ACCUSED WAR CRIMINAL INJURED IN GOVERNMENT RAID.

"The Berovian government announced today that accused war criminal, General Anton 'the Stork' Zarkov, escaped capture during a raid on his mountain hideout by Berovian soldiers.

"Just before dawn a crack unit of Berovian soldiers, acting on a tip, moved in on a farmhouse near the remote mountain village of Sotram where General Zarkov was hiding. They engaged the general's heavily armed supporters in a firefight that lasted for several hours. By the time government forces prevailed, General Zarkov had fled. The accused war criminal was reportedly shot during the battle but the extent of his injuries is unknown.

"General Zarkov is believed to have escaped into an elaborate network of caves built by the Berovian resistance during World War II. A government spokesman said that a massive manhunt was underway but acknowledged that the authorities faced a difficult task."

Alex stared at the computer screen, feeling sick to his stomach. It had taken them all this time to find the Stork. They had their chance. And they blew it.

CHAPTER THIRTY-ONE

Alex stepped off the bus at ten o'clock the next morning and hurried across the street to the travel agency. The rain pounded on his umbrella. Even by Vancouver standards, the weather this January had been abysmal. It had started raining on New Year's Day and hadn't let up for fifteen straight days.

"I need the Sarno hotel confirmation," Roman bellowed before Alex even had a chance to sit down at his desk, the demand setting the tone for the day. The second tour to Berovia and Maldania was leaving in two days and there were a million details to take care of.

Alex was happy to have the distraction. It kept him from dwelling on the Stork's narrow escape. It drove him crazy to think that the government had come so close to catching one of his father's murderers after all this time, only to have him slip through their fingers.

He was working on the trip itinerary when Peter Jurak arrived, carrying an enormous bouquet of roses.

"Bonjour," he said in an atrocious French accent. He walked to Greta's desk, knelt down, and gave her the flowers with a flourish.

"Are these supposed to make me forgive you for abandoning me?" Greta joked. Peter was headed to Hungary to work on *Vampire Killers 4*.

"No," Peter said, "but this is." He handed her an airline

ticket. She looked inside.

"Paris. Are you serious?" she asked.

"*Mais oui.* We leave Friday. I already cleared it with Roman."

"I told him it was okay as long as he promised not to tell Sophia," Roman said from the doorway to his office. "Guys like him make the rest of us look bad."

"What about the shoot?" Greta asked.

"It was cancelled," Peter said.

"We are going to have such a great time," Greta said enthusiastically. "The cafés, the art galleries, the Eiffel Tower."

"The Eiffel Tower's in Paris?" Peter asked in mock surprise.

Greta laughed, as if it was the funniest thing she'd ever heard. *I guess that's what being in love does to you*, Alex thought. *Not that you'll ever know*, the Voice commented.

Just before noon, Roman walked out of his office with a man with a neatly trimmed grey beard. "If you have any more questions, you've got my number," he said.

The two men shook hands. Tomas came out of his office as the man was walking out the door. "Was that Don Bridger?"

"Yeah. *The Sun*'s going to run a front-page story in the features section on Saturday. The media is eating this up."

"Told you they would," Tomas said. "I need the waiting list for the tour," he said to Alex, addressing him because Lara was at muay Thai practice.

"Right away, boss," Alex said. Tomas looked at him but didn't say anything.

"What's up?" Roman asked.

"You know Bill Novak, right?"

"Sure. I've known Bill for years."

"He had to cancel. He broke his arm playing basketball last night. He'll be in a cast for six weeks."

"What a shame." Roman turned to Alex. "Call Mr. Novak and get his doctor's name and contact info. You'll have to send him a medical insurance claim form so that Mr. Novak can get reimbursed by the insurance company."

"I'll take care of it," Tomas said, much to Alex's surprise. "If I find somebody to replace Bill," he said to Roman, "we split the fee fifty-fifty, right?"

"That's the deal," Roman said.

"What are they talking about?" Alex asked Greta after Tomas and Roman returned to their offices.

"The insurance company covers the cost for the guy who cancelled so Boris gets paid whether anybody takes his place or not," Greta explained, "which means the agency gets to keep the entire fee if they find a replacement. Tomas gets half, Roman gets half."

At about three o'clock an enthusiastic "Yes!" could be heard coming from Tomas's office. A few seconds later Tomas emerged.

"Get someone?" Greta asked.

"Yes. Paid the full price, too," Tomas said, a big smile on his face. Nothing made Tomas happier than making some coin.

Lara arrived at one thirty, straight from practice. Her hair was still wet from her shower.

"Get all your homework done?" she asked sarcastically as she sat down at her desk.

"Yeah. Thanks for asking."

"You can't keep everything all bottled up inside, Alex," Lara said. There was no sarcasm in her voice this time. Just concern.

"Whatever."

"I'm worried about you."

"I'm fine."

"I've never seen you like this."

"I said I was fine." He met her gaze to show he meant it.

"No, you're not," she said firmly. "Look, Alex," she said, her voice softening, "I know you're going through a rough time but you don't have to go through it alone. It helps to talk about it."

"Just let it go, Lara. Okay? Just let it go."

"Whatever you want," Lara said in disgust.

Alex and Lara didn't exchange another word until the end of the day. The conversation wasn't exactly scintillating.

"See you later," Lara said.

"See you later."

Alex watched Lara leave and then got his hockey bag out of the closet. It was time to go to practice. Given the choice, he'd rather get jabbed in the eye with a hot needle.

CHAPTER THIRTY-TWO

Alex lay in bed wishing he could stay there all day. He had been wrong about the two weeks following the Hollyburn tournament being the most miserable of his life. The next two weeks had been even worse.

He dragged himself out of bed and checked the Twitter feed. He didn't expect there to be any news and there wasn't. The Snowman had apparently vanished into thin air. As for the Stork, two days following the unsuccessful raid on his hideout, a Berovian newspaper reported that he had been fatally injured in the battle. That rumor was laid to rest the following day when his supporters released a picture of the general, a smirk on his face as he held that day's newspaper up to the camera to prove the photo was current. Aside from the cast on his broken leg, he was in perfect condition.

The Stork's injury meant he was most likely still in Berovia, but despite a thorough search of the network of caves in the mountains, the government had come up empty. They were back to where they had been before the raid. Nowhere.

The authorities continued to claim it was only a matter of time until the Stork was caught but Alex knew that was a load of crap. They had about as much chance of finding him as … as what? *As you do of getting off the bench?* the Voice suggested, scoring a direct hit.

Richmond had won three more games following the victory over West Van, and with each victory Earl Bales's confidence in himself, and the team's confidence in him, rocketed upward. Bales's performance aside, if Coach Hampton had any thoughts of putting Alex back in the starting lineup, his pathetic play during practice would have put an end to them. He was playing scared, praying that the puck would either hit him or miss the net.

Alex felt as if he were adrift in the middle of the ocean, on a raft without a paddle. Being a hockey player, a talented hockey player, was the cornerstone of his identity. It was how he defined himself. It was what set him apart. It was what made him feel special. All that was gone. He no longer knew who he was.

He had never been so depressed. Every night he went to bed thinking he'd hit rock bottom, but every morning he woke up feeling worse than the day before. Today was no exception. He dreaded the thought of going to practice, of humiliating himself once again in front of his teammates, of being reminded of how far he'd sunk. *You don't need to put yourself through this*, the Voice commiserated. *Why make yourself miserable?*

Alex got down on the floor. After seven push-ups something snapped. He lay on his stomach, unable to muster up the energy to continue. What was the point? *There is none*, the Voice agreed.

"Screw it," he said aloud. The streak had to end sometime. Now was as good a time as any. He got dressed and went downstairs.

Anna was in the kitchen when Alex entered. Sunlight streamed through the window.

"Morning, dude," Anna said.

"Morning," he grunted.

"How did you sleep?"

"Fine."

"Looks like it's going to be a beautiful day."

"Yeah," Alex said with a distinct lack of enthusiasm. He poured himself a bowl of cereal.

Anna looked at him, a worried expression on her face, but she didn't bother trying to get him to talk. She'd already tried that a number of times in the past month and he'd made it abundantly clear that he wasn't interested. He'd always been able to talk to her about stuff in the past but this was different. He had lost his mojo and nothing she could say was going to help him get it back.

"What time is practice today?" she asked.

"Five o'clock." The mere thought of going to practice bummed him out. *Why am I putting myself through this?* he asked himself. *Good question,* said the Voice. Just being in the arena was a painful reminder of how far he'd fallen. And the way he saw it, there was only one way to make the pain go away.

"Morning, dude," Anna said as Stefan came into the kitchen.

Alex and Stefan looked at each other but neither spoke. Alex's relationship with his brother was another thing in his life that had gone to shit. Stefan had reached out to him after the Hollyburn tournament, but he'd frozen him out just like he had Anna and Lara. He and his brother hadn't said more than "hey" to each other in weeks.

Alex remembered how excited he'd been when they found each other. He knew then that his life would never be the same again. His English teacher would call that ironic. His life hadn't been the same, but not in the way he'd thought.

Alex knew it wasn't Stefan's fault that his life had fallen

177

apart. It wasn't his fault that he was a better goalie than Alex. Or that Alex had choked in the biggest game of his life. Or that he wasn't going to get a scholarship offer to Minnesota, or to any other school. The only thing Alex was better at than Stefan was feeling sorry for himself. If they gave a scholarship for that, he'd be at the top of every recruiter's list.

He bolted down his cereal as quickly as he could and made his escape. As he walked into the hallway the mail came through the slot in the door.

"Can you bring the mail?" Anna called.

Alex sorted through it on his way back to the kitchen. There was a letter for Stefan from the Athletics Department at the University of Minnesota. He stopped and stared at the envelope. *This is perfect*, he thought. *The freaking icing on the freaking cake.*

He handed the letter to Stefan and the rest of the mail to Anna. When Stefan saw who the sender was, he glanced at Alex and then put the letter on the table, unopened.

"Aren't you going to open it?" Alex asked.

"I'll open it later," Stefan said.

"Open it now," Alex demanded.

"Don't be a dick," Stefan said.

Alex ripped open the envelope and started reading the letter. "Dear Stefan: It gives me great pleasure to offer you a full scholarship to play hockey at the University of Minnesota. The scholarship will cover the cost of room, board, books, tuition, and ..."

"Give me that," Anna said. She snatched the letter out of his hand.

"Congratulations, bro," Alex said to Stefan. He held his fist out. Stefan ignored it.

"Stop it," Anna said.

"What's the problem?" Alex said. "I'm just congratulating golden boy here." He held his fist out again. Stefan shook his head in disgust. "You've come a long way from Maldania, dude."

The goading finally got to Stefan. "Don't get mad at me because you choked ... dude," he said. He sarcastically put his fist out. Alex slapped it away and walked out of the kitchen.

CHAPTER THIRTY-THREE

The school day seemed to last forever. Alex would have been hard-pressed to name the classes he'd attended, let alone the subject matter they'd covered. All he could think about was going to the arena to tell Coach Hampton he was quitting. Then maybe, just maybe, the nightmare would end.

When the bell rang at the end of his last class, Alex hurried to his locker, collected the books he would need that night, and headed for the front door. Lara came up beside him.

"How's it going?" she asked.

"It's going."

"Don't you have a practice today?"

"Yeah."

"Where's your stuff?"

"At home." Lara looked at him quizzically. "I've had it," he said. "I'm quitting."

"What?" Lara looked at him in shock. "You want to talk about it?"

"Not really." They went through the front door, down the steps, and across the street to the bus stop. "It's no fun anymore," Alex said finally.

"I know it's got to be tough to be sitting on the bench after being a starter all these years, but there's only a month left in the season. Don't you think you should just gut it out?"

"What's the point?"

"The team might need you. What if Bales starts playing poorly? Or gets injured?"

"They'll figure something out. They can bring up someone from Bantam."

"Someone from Bantam?" Lara said incredulously. "Are you for real?"

"Anybody would be better than me. You wouldn't believe how bad I've been playing, even in practice. I couldn't stop your grandmother."

"Hey, don't knock Grandma," Lara joked. "She's got a wicked slapshot." Alex smiled weakly. "Are you really sure you want to do this?"

"You don't know what it's like, Lara. I hate going to practice. I don't even want to get into the game. You've seen the way I've been the last few weeks."

"You *have* been a mess," she agreed, a little too quickly for his liking. "Why don't you talk to the coach before you do anything?"

"There's nothing he can do."

"I'm your friend, Alex. You know I'll support you, whatever you decide," Lara said. "If playing hockey is making you this unhappy, then you won't be doing yourself or your teammates a favor by staying on the team. But it sounds like the problem isn't hockey, it's how you feel about yourself, and quitting the team's not going to change that."

"What makes you such an expert?" he asked. The bus turned the corner and headed toward them.

"Maybe you'll feel better tonight if you quit," Lara said as the bus pulled up, "but ask yourself if you're going to feel better tomorrow. And the day after that. And the day after that." The doors swung open.

"I guess I'll find out," Alex said, stepping onto the bus. He walked to the back. Through the rear window he saw Lara looking in his direction. He didn't care what she said. She had no idea how he felt. Nobody did. A month might not seem like a long time when you were looking at a calendar. But when you were in hell, it was an eternity.

He sat down in the last row. He had better things to do with his time than hang out in a hockey arena feeling like a useless turd. He hoped Coach Hampton wouldn't try to talk him out of it. He wanted to get out of there before any of his teammates arrived. He felt shitty about quitting on them, but like Lara said, if he felt this bad he wouldn't be doing them any favors by sticking around. He would call Kenny tonight. He deserved an explanation.

Maybe you'll feel better tonight if you quit, but ask yourself if you're going to feel better tomorrow. Lara's words bounced around inside his head. She should mind her own business, he thought. He stared out the window. This time tomorrow he'd be a free man. He'd be able to do anything he wanted to do. Anything.

He thought about that for a couple of minutes. Then he got to his feet and pushed the stop request button.

Alex was twenty minutes late for practice by the time he got to the arena after going home to retrieve his gear.

"Where were you?" Kenny Nelson asked when he stepped out onto the ice.

"Getting my shit together."

Hampton didn't say a word but Alex knew there would be a price to pay for being late, and he paid it when practice ended. Thirty minutes of wind sprints in full gear that left him lying on the ice gasping for breath—and feeling better than he had in a long, long time.

Alex went upstairs when he got home. He stopped at the doorway to Stefan's room. Stefan was at his desk, doing his homework. He knew Alex was there but he didn't look up. Alex knocked on the doorframe. Stefan finally looked at him.

"Got a minute?" Alex asked. Stefan shrugged. "How's it going?"

"I'm okay," Stefan said coolly.

"I'm sorry about those things I said today. I didn't mean them." Stefan didn't say anything. "I know I've been a dick the past few weeks." Stefan didn't bother denying it. "I'm sorry. You didn't deserve it."

"No worries. I know you've been stressed out."

After he apologized, Alex explained what had happened—the whole sorry story of how everything went off the rails after he choked in the tournament final. "I couldn't handle the fact that you were a better goalie than me," he said. Stefan didn't bother denying that either. "I lost my mojo." Stefan looked at him quizzically. "My confidence," Alex explained. Then Alex told his brother how close he'd come to quitting the team.

"That would have been a big mistake," Stefan said.

"Yeah. If it wasn't for Lara, I would have quit," he said. "I owe her."

"You do. Big time."

"So we're good?" Alex asked.

"We're good."

"See you tomorrow," Alex said.

"Hey," Stefan said when Alex got to the doorway. Alex turned around. "Don't worry, bro. You'll get it back."

"Get what back?"

"Your jomo."

"Mojo," Alex said with a laugh.

"Mojo."

The first thing Alex did when he got back to his room was call Lara and thank her for being such a good friend. Then he got down on the floor and did one hundred and one push-ups.

CHAPTER THIRTY-FOUR

"Have you decided what school you're going to go to?" Alex asked Stefan as they joined the crowd filing into the Rogers Arena for the Vancouver Canucks game against the Boston Bruins.

In the three weeks since Stefan had received the scholarship offer from the University of Minnesota, most of the other top colleges in the States had followed suit, and the pile of letters on his desk was getting higher day by day.

"Right now I'm leaning to Denver or Boston University," Stefan answered.

"I meant it when I said it's cool if you want to go to Minnesota," Alex said.

"I know you did," Stefan said, "but their starting goalie has two years of school left and I don't want to sit on the bench that long. Denver and BU are both losing their starter."

"That makes sense." It hadn't been easy but Alex had finally come to accept that his brother was a better goalie than he was without feeling like the earth was going to split open and swallow him up. That didn't mean he wasn't envious of Stefan's success. It was only natural to be jealous that his brother was living out his dream, but he had his feelings pretty much in check. The key was realizing that it was pointless to compare himself to Stefan. That had been the root cause of his problem. He came out on the short end of the comparison and that, for reasons he still didn't fully understand, had caused him to doubt his own ability. It was stupid, he realized now. His talent as a goalie was one thing, Stefan's was another, and the two had nothing to do with each other. Stefan was great, no doubt about that, but he was pretty damn good himself.

Once he'd gotten his brother out of his head, Alex had been able to focus on his own game and it wasn't long until he was playing like the Alex of old. Unfortunately, Earl Bales had continued his outstanding play, which meant that Alex's butt was still firmly planted on the bench, leaving him feeling like Wally Pipp after Lou Gehrig took his place in the Yankees' starting lineup.

The only thing that had changed was his attitude. He was no longer happy about being benched. He felt a lot better knowing that his competitive juices were flowing again, but the flip side was that his frustration was mounting game by game. He was chomping at the bit to get some ice time so he could prove, to himself and to everyone else, that he was back. But as well as he was playing in practice, Alex was plagued by a nagging doubt that kept coming to the surface, like a relentless itch. And until he proved himself in a real game, that itch wasn't going away. And with only two weeks left in the season, it didn't look like he was going to get a chance to scratch it.

With a minute left in the game, the Canucks were clinging to a 3–2 lead over Boston. The Bruins were on the attack, desperately looking for the equalizer, but they couldn't get the puck past Lou Roberts and the Canucks held on for the victory.

"What a great game," Stefan said enthusiastically. "The

Wall was unbelievable," he added, using his nickname for Lou Roberts.

Alex nodded. It was the first NHL game his brother had ever been to and his excitement was so infectious that Alex almost felt as if it were his first time as well.

"I can't believe how big and fast the players are. You don't see that on TV."

"It helps to be sitting here," Alex said. The tickets—in the fifth row, between center ice and the blue line—were a birthday present from Anna. The two of them had cleaned up this year. Boris had given them a top-of-the-line table hockey game, and Roman had given them each the latest smart phone, which they had programmed with just about every app that had ever been invented.

The three stars of the game took their victory laps. "And the first star, from the Vancouver Canucks, number 33, Lou Roberts," the announcer boomed.

"Lou, Lou," the crowd roared as Roberts skated out onto the ice.

"That could be you out there one day," Alex said.

"Yeah, right," Stefan snorted. "I don't know what you're on, but I'll take some of it." They stood up and joined the traffic jam of fans heading for the exits. "Do you really think I'm good enough to play in the NHL?" he asked a few moments later. There was a hesitation in his voice that Alex had never heard before, a hesitation that revealed how much hockey mattered to him.

"You've got a shot," Alex said. "That's all I'm saying." Earlier that week *College Hockey Magazine* had ranked Stefan as one of the top ten high school goalies in North America. It was a long way from that to the NHL, but Stefan was something special. There was no doubt about that.

Stefan beamed. Alex knew it meant a lot to his brother

to hear him say what he'd just said. It felt good to be able to say it, even if it did hurt a little.

"Just remember," Alex said, "if you do make it, I expect a pair of season tickets. Anywhere in this section will be fine."

"I'm sorry," Stefan said. "Do I know you?"

They walked up the aisle and into the main corridor. Stefan's phone rang. "Hey, babe," he said, his face lighting up. "We're just leaving. I'll be there in a half hour … I gotta pee," Stefan said after he hung up. He disappeared into the washroom.

As Alex was waiting for his brother, he saw Roman heading his way with a tall, thin man who towered over the other fans streaming out of the arena.

"Hey, Alex. How's it going?" Roman asked.

"Hi, Uncle Roman," Alex said.

"What a game," Roman said. "Bill Novak. Alex Petrovic," he said, making the introductions. "My nephew," he added.

Alex looked up at Bill. Way up. The guy had to be at least six eight.

"You're the hockey player, right?" Bill said after they shook hands.

Alex nodded. *I used to be*, he thought.

"You're looking at the next Mike Barkich," Roman said. Alex gave an appropriately modest nod. There was no point correcting him. "Bill's going on the next tour to Berovia and Maldania. He had to cancel last time."

"You're the guy who broke his arm playing basketball," Alex said, making the connection.

"Just got the cast off," Bill said.

"Bill played college ball in the States," Roman said.

"That was a long time ago," Bill said. "Back when I had

a full head of hair." He rubbed his scalp. His grey hair, what was left of it, was cut short.

"You should have seen this guy play," Roman said. "Great shooter. And he never met a shot he didn't like," he joked.

"Where did you play?" Alex asked.

"Four years at Washington State. Spent most of my time on the bench. I'm still picking the splinters out of my butt." Alex laughed. *I can relate to that.*

"Alex may be going on the tour, too," Roman said. "When do you find out?" he asked Alex.

"In two weeks. If we win the league championship, we'll be practicing for the provincials," he explained to Bill.

"My cousin's daughter, Lara, is going, too," Roman said.

"It will be great to have some young people there. Although I'm sure you'd rather be playing hockey," Bill said to Alex. "Good luck."

"Thanks," Alex said, although he wasn't actually sure he wanted the team to make it to the provincials. He was glad he hadn't quit, but sitting on the bench was sheer torture and he had no desire to prolong the agony.

Of course, if things didn't work out the way he hoped with Lara, the trip to Berovia and Maldania could turn out to be torture of a different kind. He still hadn't told her how he felt about her. His feelings for her had resurfaced once his depression lifted, but by then she had started preparing for the national championships. She had stopped working at the travel agency and was training twice a day, seven days a week. He couldn't remember the last time they'd had a chance to say more than hello to each other.

The national championships would be over in two weeks. He would tell her then.

CHAPTER THIRTY-FIVE

Alex never did get to scratch his itch. Two weeks after the
Canucks game against Boston he was in his familiar place
on the end of the bench as the clock wound down in the
league championship game. When the final buzzer
sounded, West Van had a 3–2 win and a berth in the
provincial championships.

The Cougars' bench was as silent as a tomb. From the
first day of practice the team had a single goal: winning the
league championship. The dejected look on their faces
showed how much it hurt to come so close to the prize,
only to have it slip away.

"Good luck in the provincials," Alex said to each West
Van player as they shook hands at center ice after the game.
Stefan was at the end of the West Van line. "Great game,
bro," Alex said. "You were the difference."

"Thanks," Stefan said. The two brothers looked at each
other. Alex knew they were both remembering the first
time they met, nine months earlier at the TelCel Cup. So
much had happened since then. They hugged briefly and
skated away. When Alex got back to his bench, he turned
and looked across the ice. Stefan was standing by his
bench. They saluted each other with their goalie masks.

The players were still in their uniforms when Coach
Hampton came into the room twenty minutes later, as if

leaving them on meant they didn't have to acknowledge that the season was over.

"Nobody in this room has any reason to hang his head," the coach said. "I know you wanted to win the championship, but don't make the mistake of thinking the season was a failure because we came up short. Life doesn't always work out the way we want. All you can do is go out there and give 100 percent. You did that, and you did it all season long. I'm proud of every person in this room. It's been a privilege to coach you guys."

The coach went around the room, shaking hands and saying a few words to every player.

"I guess you're glad this is all over," he said when he got to Alex. Alex shrugged. There was no point denying it. "I know things didn't turn out the way you were hoping, but I want you to know that I admire the way you handled the situation."

"Thanks." He wondered if the coach would say the same thing if he knew how close he came to quitting.

"To tell you the truth, for a while there I didn't think you were going to stick it out," Hampton said, as if he'd read Alex's mind, "but I was dead wrong about that." *Not exactly dead wrong*, Alex thought. "You showed a lot of character."

"Thanks," Alex said again.

"We would have won if you'd been playing," Kenny Nelson whispered after the coach moved on.

"You can't blame Earl," Alex said, even though Kenny was voicing his secret belief. All three West Van goals came on rebounds of shots Earl should have been able to smother. On the other hand, he made four or five outstanding saves that Alex couldn't say with certainty he would have made. He sure would have liked the chance, though.

After he changed into his street clothes he went around the room and said his goodbyes. One after another his teammates echoed Coach Hampton's sentiments. They understood what Alex had gone through in a way that only athletes could. He'd earned their respect for the way he'd gutted it out. As disappointed as he was with the way things had turned out, it meant a lot to get that kind of recognition from his teammates.

Even Mike Leonard got in on the act. "You can play on my team any time, Petrovic," was the way he put it.

Neil Daniels came up to him as he hoisted his hockey bag over his shoulder. "Thanks, Alex," he said. "For everything."

Alex took a final look around before he walked out of the locker room. He had shared a lot with these guys over the last seven months. They had celebrated victories and commiserated over defeats. Alex knew he would miss the camaraderie. But he was still glad the season was over.

Alex went straight from the rink to Fraserview Hall, where Lara was fighting in the finals of the national muay Thai championships.

It was a knockdown drag-out fight between two evenly matched competitors from start to finish. With the final round drawing to a close, Lara and her opponent from Cape Breton, Nova Scotia, stood toe-to-toe slugging it out. Both girls were exhausted. "Come on, Lara," Alex yelled, his voice hoarse. He had been on his feet, urging her on, for the entire fight.

Lara fought through the fatigue and mounted one final flurry that put her opponent back on her heels. When the bell rang she and her opponent hugged each other before going to their corners to await the judges' decision. Alex nervously snapped the rubber band on his wrist. He thought Lara had the edge but it had been a close fight and the decision could go either way.

The referee called both girls into the middle of the ring. He stood between them, holding their arms. "In the junior women's K1 lightweight title fight, the winner, by a split decision, is …"—the announcer waited a moment to heighten the suspense—"Lara Wellington from Vancouver, British Columbia."

"Yes!" Alex roared. He ran down the bleacher steps and jumped into the ring to congratulate her, along with her parents and teammates. He wrapped Lara in a bear hug and swung her around. He felt as happy as if he'd won the national championship himself.

Lara's parents took everyone out to dinner to celebrate her victory.

"Right, right," Alex said to something one of Lara's teammates was saying, but he wasn't really paying attention. He was looking at Lara. His eyes hadn't strayed from her during the entire meal. She was sitting at the other end of the table, beside her parents and her coach. She smiled at something her coach said. *She is so beautiful*, he thought. His heart ached with desire. He knew he would be devastated if she didn't feel the same way about him as he did about her. The tour to Berovia and Maldania was leaving the next morning, and he had decided to tell her how he felt when they arrived. It would be the first chance they would have to be alone.

"National Champ," Alex said when he finally got a chance to talk to Lara. They were at the dessert table. "I don't know anybody else who can say that."

"Thanks, Alex," Lara said.

"It's an incredible accomplishment," he said. "I'm really proud of you."

"Thanks," she said again. She put a slice of carrot cake on her already overflowing plate, then caught him staring at it.

"I'm moving up a weight class next year," she joked.

"Maybe a couple," he said.

"You guys must be excited about tomorrow," Lara's mother said as she joined them.

"Yeah," they both answered.

"You're going to have a great time," Lara's mother said. She put a piece of chocolate mousse cake on a plate. "I might as well put this straight on my hips," she said with a laugh.

Alex laughed but his mind was elsewhere.

CHAPTER THIRTY-SIX

"You worry too much," Stefan said to Alex as they sat in his bedroom, waiting for Anna to take Alex to the airport. "Lara really likes you."

"But does she like me like that?"

"Trust your big brother, man. She's into you." He opened his desk drawer and handed Alex a small gift-wrapped package. "I got you something for the trip."

"Thanks," Alex said. He opened the package. It was a box of condoms. "Very funny."

"It's no joke, man. You're going to need them."

He put the package on the desk. "I don't want to jinx things."

"Suit yourself," Stefan said. He put the condoms back in the desk drawer.

"I know San Marco is on the itinerary," Anna said as she drove Alex to the airport, "but that doesn't mean you have to go."

"I want to go," Alex said. He knew it would be painful to stand in the building where his father was killed, but even though he had never known him, in a strange way he felt it was his duty as a son. His father was a brave and daring man. He proved that by fighting for Anna, and by saving Stefan's life. His father had never been buried. Going to the church would be like visiting the cemetery, a way to show his respect.

Alex wondered where the Stork and the Snowman were. By now the Stork's broken leg would have healed, and there would be no reason for him to stay in Berovia. Alex imagined the two men lying on a beach on a remote island where nobody had ever heard of Berovia or Maldania, drinking slivovitz and reminiscing about the good old days. Like the time they burned that church down. *To good times. Dos Prosta. Clink. Clink.*

Anna pulled up at the passenger drop-off for international flights at the Vancouver International Airport. She and Alex got out of the car. Alex took his suitcase out of the trunk. "I know the past few months have been difficult," she said. "I'm proud of the way you've handled everything. Your dad would be proud of you, too." She hugged him goodbye. "I'm going to miss you, dude."

"I'm going to miss you, too, Anna."

Roman was talking to Bill Novak near the check-in counter when Alex walked into the terminal. Roman looked like a child beside him. Lara was nearby, handing orange luggage tags to the tour group members and ticking their names off a list on a clipboard.

"Hey," she said as Alex walked up to her.

"Hey." She looked fantastic.

"Is that everyone?" Roman asked Lara.

"Yes."

"I thought Peter and Greta were coming with us," Alex said. Peter had proposed to Greta the week before and was taking her to Berovia to meet his parents.

"They needed Peter on the set for another day," Roman said. "They're flying out tomorrow."

"Guess you didn't make the provincials," Bill Novak said to Alex. "That's too bad." Alex shrugged, then glanced involuntarily at Lara. "Or not."

Or not. That would depend on what Lara said when he told her how he felt.

Alex and Lara sat beside each other on the plane, watching the city recede into the distance as they climbed higher and higher. As soon as they were above the clouds, Lara opened her knapsack and took out her biology textbook. "I hate it when teachers give you homework over the holidays," she said. "Why do they do that?"

"Because they're sad and bitter people whose only joy in life is causing misery to others."

"That must be it," she said with a laugh as she opened her textbook.

Alex watched her as he pretended to look out the window. It took all his willpower to stop himself from telling her how he felt, but he knew he had to wait until they were alone. Ten hours on the plane and two more to clear customs and get to the hotel. It was going to be a long twelve hours. And a long two weeks if she said she didn't think of him the same way.

If she said she just wanted to be friends, he'd nod and say that was fine, but he knew that wasn't possible. Whatever happened, their friendship, as it existed, was over. Things could never go back to the way they were. He glanced at her. Her head was buried in her textbook. Yup. It was going to be a long twelve hours.

He managed to get a couple of hours of homework done before he dozed off. When he woke up, Lara was asleep, her head on his shoulder. A few loose strands of her hair tickled his cheek. He gently tucked them against her head. A smile flitted across her face.

He wondered what he should say to her. He knew what

he wanted to say, more or less; he just wasn't sure exactly how he should say it. *I'm in love with you.* It was direct, and it was the truth, but there was no way he could say that. It would probably just freak her out. He ran through a few other scenarios before he came up with one he liked. *I know we've been friends for a long time, but my feelings for you have changed.* Plain and simple. The key was to find the right moment.

Bill Novak came out of the washroom and walked down the aisle toward him. He was bent over at the waist so his head wouldn't hit the ceiling. He smiled at Alex and sat down in the empty seat across the aisle, his knees tucked under his chin.

"What do you think of the Canucks' chances this year?" he asked.

"If Lou keeps playing the way he's playing, they're going to be tough to beat."

"Spoken like a true goalie," Bill said.

The two of them talked hockey for the next couple of hours, until the pilot announced that the plane would be landing soon and asked everyone to return to their seats.

Two hours later, just after noon local time, Alex and Lara were wheeling their suitcases off the elevator on the twelfth floor of the Hotel Excelsior in Grabel, the capital of Maldania.

"What room are you in?" Alex asked.

Lara checked her key card. "1212."

"I'm in 1210." Right next door.

They got to Lara's room first. She swiped her card and opened the door. "What time are we meeting Boris?" she asked.

"Five thirty." Boris had invited Alex and Lara to his

house for dinner. He hadn't scheduled anything for the tour the first day so that everybody could rest up after the flight. It was three in the morning Vancouver time, and the tour group members would need the day to recover from jetlag.

"Are you tired?" he asked.

"Not really. You?"

Alex shook his head. "Want to go for a walk?"

"Sure."

Alex and Lara spent the afternoon wandering along the cobblestone streets of the Old City. It was the first trip to Europe for both of them and neither of them had seen anything like it. Narrow streets barely wide enough for two people to walk side-by-side; stone churches that were more than eight hundred years old; old men with grizzled beards playing chess and drinking coffee at sidewalk cafés. Lara took a million photos.

The Old City had been heavily damaged during the war but most of it had been rebuilt. Occasionally, however, they came across a wall pitted with bullet holes, a bombed-out house without a roof, a reminder of the dark reality that lay beneath the fairy-tale exterior.

"That's beautiful," Lara said when they turned a corner and found themselves staring at the sea through an opening in the stone wall that surrounded the Old City. They walked through the opening and onto the beach. A few locals were sunning themselves on the white sand.

They walked to the shoreline. Lara snapped another picture and then took off her shoes, rolled up her pant legs, and dipped her foot into the water.

"It's warm," she said. She walked out up to her knees.

Alex followed her into the sea. Sunbeams danced on the water. A sailboat scooted by in the distance. Lara closed her eyes and held her face toward the sun. There was nobody else around. Alex had been waiting for the right moment and this was it. *I know we've been friends for a long time*, he silently rehearsed, *but my feelings for you have changed.* Before he could get the words out of his mouth, a wave rolled in, causing Lara to lose her balance. She stumbled against him. He caught her, stopping her from falling in the water. She looked up at him, making no effort to disengage. Their eyes met. Alex hesitated, but just for a moment, and then leaned down and kissed her on the lips. Lara responded.

"I've been wanting to do that for a long time," he said when they finally separated.

"Me, too. That was nice."

"Really?" he asked, as if she might be lying.

"Maybe you'd better do it again just to make sure."

They made sure for another half hour. "We'd better get back before Boris sends out a search party," Alex said finally.

After they returned from dinner at Boris's house, they went to Lara's room and made sure some more. It was nearly midnight by the time Alex got back to his room. He'd been awake for twenty-five straight hours, but he was high as a kite. He knew there was no way he was going to fall asleep so he Skyped Stefan.

"I hate to say I told you so," his brother said when Alex brought him up to speed, "but I told you so."

Alex didn't mind one bit. "You were right," he said.

"Just so you know," Stefan said before they signed off, "*condom* is the same in Berovian as it is in English."

CHAPTER THIRTY-SEVEN

Boris led the tour group to the top of the tower of the fourteenth-century palace.

"It costs a lot to run a palace," Boris said, "but the king of Maldania had a very effective way of raising revenue. He would kidnap wealthy people and if their families didn't pay the ransom, he would make them walk off the tower. Needless to say his collection rate was very high."

Alex and Lara laughed along with everyone else as they peered over the metal railing that rimmed the tower, looking down at the jagged rocks hundreds of feet below. Lara leaned out and snapped a picture.

"You might want to consider paying me back the money I lent you yesterday," she said, putting a hand on Alex's back and pretending to push.

Alex laughed again but his thoughts were elsewhere. Things had gotten pretty hot and heavy in the week since they had their first kiss but they still hadn't had sex. It was all he could think about. He felt a little embarrassed at being so obsessed but that's the way it was. He couldn't help it. He glanced at Lara. He wished he knew what she was thinking. He was pretty sure she wanted to do it too, but he knew he was going to have to make the first move, and he was determined to make it tonight.

"Want me to take your picture?" Bill Novak asked.

"Sure." She handed him her camera. He took their

picture, and then Lara took one of him and Alex, and Alex took one of her and Bill.

"Your boy Lou didn't have such a good game yesterday," Bill said, needling Alex. The Los Angeles Kings had beaten the Canucks 5–1.

"He'll bounce back," Alex said. "He always does." *A good goalie needs a bad memory.* Alex realized he hadn't thought about the hockey season since they'd landed in Grabel. A feeling of regret at never having had the opportunity to redeem himself washed over him, but one look at Lara and he forgot all about it.

Boris led the group back down the tower and into the palace. One room looked pretty much like the next—stone floors and rugs on the walls—not that Alex was paying much attention. He was too busy trying to figure out how he could get to the pharmacy across the plaza in front of the palace before they returned to the hotel. He wished he'd taken the condoms Stefan had given him.

When the tour finally came to an end, the group gathered around Boris in the middle of the huge entrance room. "The bus to the hotel leaves in an hour," he said, his voice echoing off the thick walls. "They have a nice gift shop here or you might want to walk around the neighborhood. If you want to have a coffee and people-watch, any of the places on the plaza will do just fine. It's our last night in Maldania and the hotel is putting on a special spread for us tonight. It starts at six o'clock so don't spoil your dinner, kids." Everybody laughed.

"What do you want to do?" Alex asked Lara.

"I'm going to check out the gift shop. See if I can find something for my mother."

Yes! "Okay. I'm going to walk around for a bit. I'll catch you later."

Alex went up and down the pharmacy's four aisles twice, but there were no condoms to be found. He walked to the counter at the rear of the store. The pharmacist was a woman. *Just my luck*, he thought. There were three customers ahead of him. By the time it was his turn, two elderly ladies had lined up behind him.

"How can I help you?" the pharmacist asked in Berovian.

"Kapet kondom limo," Alex whispered. *A package of condoms, please.*

The pharmacist asked a question in Berovian but she spoke too quickly and Alex didn't understand what she saying. The two women behind him laughed. The pharmacist repeated the question, this time more slowly. "What size do you want? Regular, large, or extra large?" *You've got to be kidding*, Alex thought. He could feel his face flush with embarrassment. The pharmacist looked him up and down, as if she were sizing him up so she could help make the decision.

"Large," he said finally in Berovian.

The pharmacist reached below the counter and took out six boxes of condoms, all made by different companies. She started to explain the difference but before she finished her first sentence Alex grabbed the first box he saw.

He could feel the old ladies' eyes burning a hole in his back as he walked out of the pharmacy.

Alex Skyped Stefan when he got back to the hotel. "What do I say?" he asked when he told his brother that he was going to tell Lara he wanted to have sex with her.

"Just don't tell her it's your first time," Stefan said.

"Why not?"

"Do you think she and Jason had sex?"

"Yeah." He was almost sure of it. "What difference does that make?" Stefan let him figure it out by himself. "Right," Alex said a few seconds later. If he told Lara it was his first time, she'd feel like she had to say something. And nothing would spoil the mood more than her telling him that she'd done it with Jason.

Dinner must have been good, judging by the satisfied looks on the tour group members' faces when they walked out of the hotel restaurant, but Alex hadn't been able to eat a thing. He felt as nervous as he did before a big game.

He and Lara went up in the elevator together. When they got to Lara's room, she took out her key card. "Good night," she said. "See you in the morning." A comical look must have appeared on Alex's face because Lara burst out laughing.

"Very funny," he said.

"I thought so."

They went into the room.

"Do you want to have sex?" he blurted out after they kissed for a few minutes. The words sounded stupid. He was about to tell her that they didn't have to if she didn't want to when she nodded.

Afterward Alex told Lara about his adventures in the pharmacy.

"You are so beautiful," he said after they stopped laughing. She beamed. Then they did it again.

You finally got laid, dude, he thought when they finished. He felt embarrassed for thinking it but he couldn't stop the thought from entering his mind. What they had just done meant a lot more to him than that. He cared about Lara. He cared about her a lot. But part of him wanted to go out on the balcony and let the world know that Alex Petrovic wasn't a virgin anymore. He laughed at the image.

"What are you laughing about?" Lara asked.

"Nothing," he said. He hadn't realized he'd laughed aloud. He turned back on his side and faced her. "You are so beautiful," he said again. "I've got to stop saying that."

"Yeah. Girls hate being told that," she said with a straight face.

"You're joking, right?"

"You've got a lot to learn about girls."

You don't know the half of it. "That was my first time," he blurted out again, ignoring Stefan's advice. *Idiot,* he said to himself.

"I'm glad," she said, touching his face. "It was my first time, too. First and second."

Alex reached for her. "Have you ever heard of a hat trick?"

CHAPTER THIRTY-EIGHT

The next few days were so great—for obvious reasons—that Alex didn't think about the visit to the museum at the Church of San Marco until he boarded the bus that would take him there.

The half-hour ride took place in silence. Everybody was steeling themselves for what lay ahead. The bus parked in front of the church. The charred stone walls were still intact, a vivid reminder of what had happened. The church windows had been replaced by stained-glass images of the victims being consumed by flames. The look of agony on their faces was eerily similar to the way he had imagined it.

Alex went inside the church. Somber music played softly on the sound system. He stood in front of a glass case containing the items found in the church after the fire: keys, glasses, a crucifix, partially burned clothing. He wondered if any of them had belonged to his father.

Just being in the church, standing where his father might have stood, brought home the horror in a way that he had never felt before. He closed his eyes and tried to imagine what it was like for his father and the other victims, the panic they must have felt when the church was set on fire, the pain as the flames consumed them. He remembered reading that mothers had killed their own children so they wouldn't have to suffer anymore.

He moved from exhibit to exhibit, but he didn't take

any of it in. He was overwhelmed by sadness. After a few minutes of aimless wandering, he found himself standing in front of a picture of the Stork and the Snowman. It was the same one he'd seen on the Internet. Zarkov towering over Koralic, a gun in his left hand, the two of them laughing.

He quickly moved away. He couldn't bear to look at their faces. The next exhibit featured stories of Berovians who had sheltered Maldans during the war, ordinary men and women who had risked their lives to save strangers. The stories of these heroes, right beside the picture of the Stork and the Snowman, reminded him of the quotation from his course on genocide. "People will do anything to, or for, each other."

Candles honoring the dead flickered on a mantel in the corner. Alex lit a candle for his father and put it into a bronze candlestick. He stood and watched the flame, and thought about the father he never had a chance to know.

Lara came up beside him and took his hand in hers. She gave it a gentle squeeze that told him she knew just how he felt. He had never felt so connected to her.

"Let's get out of here," he said.

They sat on a bench in the courtyard, waiting for the other tour members to come out. Neither of them had said a word since they left the church.

Alex thought back on everything that had happened in the past year. His whole life up to now had been about hockey. It had dominated his thoughts. He wasn't sure if he was going to keep playing, but if he did he knew it would never be the obsession it had been. He didn't know what the future held in store, but he would never again define himself as a hockey player. He felt as if one chapter of his life had ended and another had begun.

He was proud of the way he dealt with the crushing of

his hockey dreams, and about confronting Mike Leonard. He had been tested, and he had found within himself an inner strength he never knew he had, an inner strength that had silenced the Voice forever.

He remembered the joy he felt when he and Stefan found each other, and the sibling rivalry that nearly ruined the relationship. They'd gotten through that and now the two of them shared an unbreakable bond that would last for the rest of their lives.

And then there was Lara. Until you experience love, he thought, you can't understand what it feels like. He'd seen people in love in the movies and read about them in books. He'd seen it in real life, too. He had thought he'd known what it felt like. But all he had known was the yearning, the desire to be in love. He hadn't known what it felt like to actually be in love, to have that yearning fulfilled. And now that he knew, he realized he had known nothing at all about love. It changed the way he felt about himself. It changed the way he looked at the world. It changed everything.

Lara's head was resting on his chest. His arm was around her shoulders. He wondered if she knew how he felt about her. He wanted to tell her, but just thinking about saying those three small words—I love you—filled him with fear, the fear that they wouldn't be returned.

He turned toward her. She looked up at him. "Are you okay?" she asked.

"I love you."

Her face lit up with a smile that made his heart soar. "I love you, too."

A few minutes later everybody filed out of the church and got back on the bus. He sat down and looked out the window at the church. He watched until it was out of sight. He felt as if he had just completed a long voyage.

CHAPTER THIRTY-NINE

Two days later, Alex and Lara wheeled their suitcases out of the hotel and handed them to the bus driver, who stowed them in the luggage compartment.

"I'll see you guys in a couple of days," Boris said. He had to stay behind to take care of some business, but he'd be in Vancouver the following week, in time for Stefan's first game in the provincial championships.

Alex and Lara got on the bus, stashed their knapsacks on the overhead shelf and sat down.

"I wish we weren't going home," Lara said.

"Me too." The last two weeks had been the best two weeks of his life. It was like he and Lara had been on their honeymoon.

The other tour members slowly filed onto the bus. Everybody was moving at half speed, still recovering from the farewell dinner the previous night. They had started off toasting Boris, and then each other, and then world peace, and they didn't run out of steam until there was nothing left to toast except the cutlery.

Bill Novak walked onto the bus, moving carefully as if he was afraid of falling.

"What do you have to say about my man Lou now?" Alex asked. Lou had recorded two shutouts in a row, propelling the Canucks into first place in their division.

Bill looked right past him and continued to the back of

the bus. He looked like shit. *He must have really tied one on,* Alex thought. Adults were weird. They were always warning kids about the dangers of alcohol but they sure didn't need much of an excuse to get drunk.

When they got to the airport, they discovered that their flight had been delayed. The first thought to cross Alex's mind was that there was another bomb threat like there had been after the first tour, but it turned out that their plane was an hour late arriving from Paris.

"Let's make a run for it," Alex said to Lara when it was time to board. They joined the lineup in front of the gate.

"I wish," Lara said. She stepped back and pointed the camera at Alex. "Say 'goodbye, Sarno.'"

"Goodbye, Sarno," Alex said as Lara snapped the picture. Bill Novak walked up behind Alex.

"Let me take one of the two of you," Lara said. Alex stood next to Bill. "Say '*vo dinya, Sarno,*'" Lara said.

"*Vo dinya, Sarno,*" Alex and Bill said at the same time.

Alex spotted Anna and Stefan as soon as he and Lara stepped through the doors at the arrivals level. Lara's mother and father were standing beside them. He and Lara looked at each other.

The honeymoon was over.

CHAPTER FORTY

"That was delicious," Lara said as she, Alex, and Stefan cleared the plates off the table.

"Thanks," Alex said.

"What time does the movie start?" Stefan asked after they'd cleaned up the kitchen and gone into the living room. The three of them were going to the opening of the new Johnny Chin movie at the Cineplex on West Pender.

"Nine thirty," Alex said. "Too bad Emma isn't here," he said to Stefan. "When's she coming back?" Emma had spent March break with her grandmother in Victoria.

"The day after tomorrow."

"You want to see the pictures from the trip?" Lara asked Stefan.

"Sure."

Lara opened her computer. She and Stefan sat down on the couch. Alex sat on Lara's other side, opened his computer, and went to his Facebook page. He'd seen the photos on the flight home.

"These are the ones we took at your house when Boris had us over for dinner," Lara said.

"Very funny," Stefan said. He was looking at a picture of his bedroom. Alex and Lara had put a teddy bear on his pillow as a joke.

"We thought so," Lara said. "Boris said you slept with it until you were …"

211

"Fifteen," Alex interrupted.

"Ha, ha."

Alex scrolled through the usual assortment of photos and messages and then checked his email. There was a Twitter alert from the War Crimes Tribunal from the day before, the day they'd flown home. The link led to a newspaper article.

The headline read: IT WAS ZARKOV, WITNESS INSISTS.

"Shortly after ten o'clock last night Milos Felden, a custodian at the Grand Hotel in the village of Barnok, called police and reported that he had seen accused war criminal General Anton Zarkov and two other men in one of the hotel rooms. But when officers from Number Two Division in Sarno, the nearest police station, arrived an hour later, the room was empty.

"The hotel receptionist and a guest told police that they had seen a very tall, thin man leave the hotel in the company of two other men, but they were positive that it was not the general, whose face is well known throughout the country.

"'Both witnesses said that the man they saw had short grey hair and a receding hairline, and that he was at least ten years younger than the general,' a police spokesman said. They stated that they had an unobstructed view of the man and that his face was unscarred. As you know, General Zarkov is not.'" Alex didn't have to look at Zarkov's picture to remember the jagged scar that ran from just below his ear to his jaw.

"Mr. Felden insisted the two witnesses were lying. 'I know who I saw. It was Zarkov.' He accused the police of collaborating in a cover-up to prevent him from claiming the $500,000 reward offered for information leading to the general's arrest."

Another nutcase, Alex thought. He moved on to the hockey scores. The Canucks had defeated Montreal 3–0, their third win in a row.

"The Wall shut out the Canadiens last night," Alex said. "That's three in a row."

"How many does that give him for the season?"

"Eight." Alex wondered if the custodian actually thought he'd seen the Stork, or if he had flat out lied. If that was the case, he really was nuts.

"That's the palace in Grabel," Lara said, "where the king made people walk off the tower if their families wouldn't pay the ransom. You must have been there."

"Many times. Who's that guy with Alex?" Stefan asked.

Alex leaned over and took a look at the picture. "Bill Novak."

"You look like a little boy beside him," Stefan said. "How tall is he?"

"About six eight," Alex said. "He played ball at Washington State."

Lara clicked on the next picture. "This is our hotel in Grabel." She leaned against Alex. "They ran out of hot water the day we got there."

"The swimming pool smelled like rotten eggs," Alex said.

"And the doorman was nasty."

"Best hotel ever," Alex said.

"I'd go back there in a flash," Lara added.

"You guys are cute," Stefan said.

Alex turned back to the article on the Canucks game but thoughts of the Zarkov sighting intruded. It didn't make sense that the custodian would lie. If the man he saw wasn't Zarkov, he wouldn't get the reward. Alex reread the story.

"Let me see the picture of me and Bill," he said to Lara.
"What for?"

"Humor me." Lara shrugged and went back to the photo.

"Listen to this," Alex said. He read the article aloud, stopping after he read the key sentence: "'Both witnesses said that the man they saw had short grey hair and a receding hairline, and that he was at least ten years younger than the general.'" He pointed at Bill Novak's picture. "Remind you of anybody?"

"What are you saying?" Lara said. "That the man he saw was Bill?"

"I don't know. But how many men in Berovia match that description?"

"This happened at ten o'clock the night before last, right?" Lara said. Alex nodded. "That was our last night in Sarno. We all had dinner at the hotel. Bill was there, too. Getting shit-faced."

"I know," Alex said.

"Maybe he has an identical twin," Stefan said.

"Didn't you think Bill was acting weird yesterday?" Alex asked Lara.

"I thought he was hungover."

"Did you speak to him?"

Lara gave it a few seconds' thought, casting her mind back. "No. Not that I can remember."

"Me neither," Alex said. "Whenever I said anything, he just nodded ... Where's the picture you took of us at the airport?" Lara scrolled through the photos until she found it. "Put it beside the one from the palace," Alex said.

"Looks like the same man to me," Lara said.

Alex stared at the photos, looking at every detail, as if it were one of those puzzles where you have to find ten differences between two apparently identical pictures. "Holy shit," he said after a while.

"What?" Lara asked.

"Look at his watch."

"It's not the same watch," Stefan said.

"He's not the only person in the world to have two watches," Lara said.

"Yeah," said Alex, "but he's wearing it on his left wrist in the photo at the palace and on his right in the one at the airport."

"Zarkov's left-handed," Stefan said, his eyes widening as the realization hit him. "Left-handed people wear their watch on their right wrist."

It didn't take Alex long to find the picture of Zarkov he'd stared at so often, the one where he was standing beside the Snowman, laughing into the camera, holding a gun in his left hand. The watch on his right wrist had a silver band and a black face—just like the one in the picture taken at the airport. "That's not Bill Novak," he said, pointing at the picture from the airport. "That's the Stork."

"Peter," Lara said softly.

"Peter," echoed Alex.

"Who's Peter? What are you talking about?" Stefan asked.

"You know Peter Jurak, Roman and Tomas's friend, the guy who does makeup for the movies?" Stefan nodded. "He was in Berovia," Alex said.

"But he wasn't there to introduce Greta to his parents," Lara said. "He made up the Stork to look like Bill so they could smuggle him out of the country as part of the tour group."

"Airport security didn't give him a second look. They

waved us all through," Alex said.

It was brilliant, absolutely brilliant.

"Holy shit," Alex said again. "They got the Snowman out the same way." He turned to Stefan. "Remember when we had dinner at Lombardo's just before Christmas, the day your dad arrived?"

"Yeah."

"Remember the fat guy who came to the table? He was on the first tour."

"Yeah," Stefan said. "He was really drunk. Mom got Dad to put him a cab so he wouldn't drive home."

"When Boris mentioned the bomb threat at the airport he reacted as if he didn't know what he was talking about. He tried to cover it up by saying he was drunk. But he didn't forget about the bomb threat. He didn't know about it because he wasn't at the airport when the tour left. The Snowman took his place."

"Peter was in Sarno then, too," Lara said, her excitement rising. "Remember how everybody thought he was cheating on Greta until we found out he was visiting his cousin Iris?"

"*You* thought he was cheating."

"That was his excuse for being there," Lara continued, ignoring the correction. "He was really there to disguise the Snowman."

It all came together in a rush. Alex remembered how eager Tomas had been to do a second tour, and how pissed off he was when Boris said he couldn't do another one until after Christmas. It wasn't because he needed the money for Lina's private school. He wanted to get the Stork out of Berovia as quickly as possible.

"Bill was supposed to go on the second tour," he said. "They planned to do the switch then, but the Stork broke his leg when the government raided his hideout so he wasn't able to go on the trip."

"And when he couldn't go, Bill cancelled. He didn't really break his arm," Lara said.

"Peter was planning to be there, too, so he could disguise the Stork," Alex said. "But when Zarkov got injured, Peter said the shoot in Hungary was cancelled. He ended up taking Greta to Paris. What was the name of the movie he said he was working on?"

"*Vampire Killers 3*. Or maybe four. I can't remember."

Alex did a quick search. "There's not even a *Vampire Killers 1*," he said. "He made it all up. He just needed a reason to explain why he was going away."

The three of them looked at each other, their faces flushed with excitement.

"How are we going to prove this?" Stefan asked. The question brought them back down to earth.

"Wait a minute," Lara said. "The doctor who filled in Bill's medical claim form must have been in on it, too."

"You're right," Alex said.

"You've lost me again," Stefan said.

"Bill said he couldn't go on the tour because he broke his arm," Alex explained. "He didn't really break it, but a doctor had to fill out a medical claim form saying he did so that the insurance company would reimburse him for the cost of the tour."

"Do we know who the doctor was?" Lara asked.

"I can find out." Alex accessed his travel agency email account on his computer. He scrolled back until he found the email from the insurance company approving Bill Novak's claim. "Dr. Marcus Ratliff," Alex said. He Googled him. "He's a plastic surgeon ... And he specializes in facial reconstruction."

"Oh my God," Lara and Stefan said at the same time.

Nobody had to state the obvious. The Snowman had already been operated on. The Stork was next in line. Once Ratliff gave him a new face, the two of them would disappear forever.

Lara asked the question they were all thinking.

"What are we going to do now?"

CHAPTER FORTY-ONE

Alex turned his head from side to side, trying to get the stiffness out of his neck. He'd been sitting in the car for six hours, watching Marcus Ratliff's house on Marine Drive in Southlands. The plan they had come up with the night before was simple. Follow Ratliff and hope he would lead them to the Stork.

It had crossed Alex's mind that this was his chance to live out his fantasy movie ending, the one where he blew the Stork's head off, but now that it was within the realm of possibility, the prospect of confronting Zarkov face-to-face scared the shit out of him. He, Lara, and Stefan were all agreed. They wouldn't try to be heroes. If they found out where the Stork was hiding, they would call the police and let them take it from there.

Just before noon, Stefan got off the bus at the stop up the road. He was taking the twelve-to-six shift. Then Lara would take over.

Alex got out of the car. "Bond. James Bond," he said, tossing the car keys to Stefan.

"Which house is it?" Stefan asked.

"The one with the two black Mercs," Alex said, pointing to a mansion on the other side of the road.

"I think I'm going to be a plastic surgeon when I grow up," Stefan said.

"Call me if he leaves the house, and don't follow him

too closely," Alex said.

"Yes, James." Stefan said. The two brothers jabbed fists, then Alex walked to the bus stop.

He took the number forty-nine bus to Main Street and then got off to wait for the number three to take him to the travel agency. He was standing at the bus stop when Tomas drove up in his silver Audi.

"Get in," he said.

"I'm good," Alex said.

"Don't be stupid. Get in."

The last thing Alex wanted to do was get in the car with Tomas, knowing what he knew, but as far as Tomas was concerned the truce had held and it would have looked fishy if Alex had refused. He got in the car. Tomas had just driven off when his cellphone rang.

"Hello," he said.

A voice on the speakerphone answered in Berovian. *"Je Marco. Je slago. Node Roman?"* It's Marco. I'm leaving. Where's Roman?

"I'll call you back," Tomas said in Berovian.

A moment later Stefan texted Alex. *He's on the move.*

K, Alex texted back. Then it hit him. The timing of the call Tomas received and Stefan's text was no coincidence. Marco was a nickname for Marcus. The doctor had left his house, and Alex's guess was that he was on his way to operate on the Stork.

But what did Roman have to do with it? Was it possible his uncle was involved after all? Roman had told him that he believed the Stork and the Snowman were criminals, but he could have been lying. After all, he supported the Freedom Party, the party that had protected them all these years. Did he agree to go into business with Boris because it was a good opportunity? Or did he do it because it was the perfect way to get the two men out of Berovia?

Alex sat in shocked silence as they drove to the agency. Fortunately, Tomas had as little interest in conversation as he did. As soon as they got to the agency, Tomas disappeared into Roman's office and closed the door.

"Do you really think Uncle Roman is part of this?" Lara asked dubiously after Alex brought her up to date. "Remember what happened the last time we thought that?"

"I know," Alex said. Then he remembered seeing Roman with Bill Novak at the Canucks game. They'd known each other for years. Roman would have known that Bill could double for the Stork. He was probably the one who recruited him.

He and Lara tossed that into the mix when Roman and Tomas came out of his office. "I'll be gone all day," Roman said. "If you need me, you can get me on my cell."

Fifteen minutes later Stefan sent a text. *Heading west on hwy 1.* Alex guessed that Ratliff was going to the terminal at Horseshoe Bay. From there a ferry would take him to the Sunshine Coast. The Stork could be hiding in any one of dozens of remote communities up the coast, where people had never heard of Berovia or Maldania.

Fifteen minutes later Stefan sent another text. *Just passed Horseshoe Bay.* Ratliff wasn't taking a ferry to the Sunshine Coast. He was heading in the direction of Whistler.

"Roman has a place in Lions Bay," Lara said slowly. Lions Bay was on the way to Whistler, about a ten-minute drive from Horseshoe Bay.

"I know," Alex said. His heart sank. He'd been there once. It was the perfect location for a hiding place, up in the hills, well off the beaten track.

Twenty minutes crept by with no further word from Stefan. Suddenly a stabbing pain sliced through Alex's head, just above his left eye. A couple of seconds later it happened again. He felt a terrible sense of dread.

"Something's happened to Stefan," he said.

"How do you know?"

"I just know." He grabbed his phone and texted Stefan. *Where r u?* The seconds ticked by. No answer. Alex called Stefan's phone. It rang a few times and then went to voicemail. Alex felt woozy. He closed his eyes.

"Are you okay?"

After a few seconds the pain and wooziness went away. He nodded. "He's in trouble. Bad trouble. Give me your car keys."

"You're not going without me," Lara said. Alex started to object but the determined look on Lara's face told him he'd be wasting his breath.

CHAPTER FORTY-TWO

Forty minutes later they turned off the highway at Lions Bay. A few minutes after that they were driving along an unpaved road up in the hills toward Roman's place.

"That's it," Alex said, pointing to a simple log cabin. There were no cars in the driveway. They parked out of sight, and then circled back on foot. They snuck around to the back of the cabin and looked through a window. The cabin was dark. There was no sign of life.

"There's nobody here," Lara said.

"It doesn't mean Roman's not involved," Alex said.

"I know. But what do we do now?" Lara asked.

"I don't know," he said helplessly. Then his face brightened. "Stefan's got the 'find my phone' app," he said excitedly. It was one of the apps they had downloaded when they got the smart phones for their birthday. He navigated to the app sign-in page.

"Don't you need a password? Lara asked, stopping Alex in his tracks. Of course he did.

"Maybe it has something to with hockey," Lara suggested. Alex looked at her. *Get real.* "Doesn't really narrow it down, does it?" she said apologetically.

Stefan's password probably did have something to do with hockey, he thought. So what? His did, too. He grabbed his phone, entered his password—*LouRoberts*—and prayed that he'd be able to add one more item to the

223

list.

Log-in Failed.

He looked at the screen, stunned. He had been sure it was going to work. Stupidly sure. He tried every variation he could think of—all caps, part caps, no caps, an underscore between *Lou* and *Roberts*—but he came up empty. He fought the panic that rose up in his gut.

"Maybe it's another player," Lara said. "Who else does he like?"

There was nobody else, Alex thought. Just the Wall. *The Wall!* He typed it in the password field. "Holy shit," he said. He was in.

A few minutes later he and Lara were stopped at the foot of a driveway on Mountain Drive.

"That is it," Alex said, looking at the screen on his phone. The house wasn't visible from the driveway.

Lara drove past the driveway. A hundred or so yards farther down the road they saw Anna's car pulled over to the side. Lara parked behind it. They got out and peered into the car but everything looked normal.

They stepped into the wooded area beside the driveway, where they wouldn't be seen if somebody drove by, and walked up a rise. A short while later they reached the top. There was a cabin in the clearing. They stayed well back, making sure to keep out of sight. A black Mercedes was parked in front, along with a grey Honda Accord.

"That's Ratliff's car," Alex said, pointing to the Mercedes.

"There's a camera over the front door," Lara said. "I bet that's how they caught Stefan."

Fear was etched on both their faces as the reality of the situation hit home. Stefan was being held prisoner in the cabin by people who had killed before and wouldn't hesitate to kill again.

"Let's go back to the road and call the police," Alex whispered. Lara nodded. She wanted to get out of there as badly as he did.

Alex turned around ... and stared into the barrel of a gun. The Stork loomed over him, a grim look on his face. The jagged scar made him look like a character in a horror movie. Alex felt as if his heart was going to burst out of his chest. The Stork held out his right hand.

"Phone," he barked. Alex handed him his phone. The Stork stomped on it with the heel of a polished black shoe, grinding it into the ground. Then he pointed to the cabin with his left hand, the one that held the gun. *"Presti."* Move.

Lara was shaking with fear. Alex took her hand. It was cold as ice.

The Stork chuckled. *"Pije cade."* Nice boy.

He prodded Alex in the back with his gun. They walked up the steps and through the front door. It led to a large, open area. Off to the left, a man with slicked-back hair sat in front of a bank of monitors, his back to them. One of the monitors showed the entrance to the driveway. They had seen Alex and Lara coming.

The man turned around. He had a bushy moustache. It was the man Tomas had met in the restaurant way back when, the guy whose brother needed a fake passport.

"I have to go now," the man said in Berovian. "I'll be back tomorrow."

"Okay, Roman. See you later."

Roman. As soon as he heard the name Alex realized his uncle had nothing to do with this. Given the circumstances, it was small consolation.

A toilet flushed. A few seconds later a fat man came out of a room off the hallway. He had short blond hair, protruding ears, and a narrow nose. Nobody would know it was the Snowman, not even if he walked down the main street in Sarno singing the national anthem.

He looked at Alex and Lara, shaking his head as if they were the two stupidest people he'd ever seen. Alex was inclined to agree.

The Stork and the Snowman led them down a hallway. The kitchen was at the far end. It had been converted into an operating room. There was a stretcher near the far wall, beside a stand with a powerful light, like the kind in a dentist's office. A man wearing a doctor's gown was at the stove, sterilizing surgical instruments in a pot of boiling water. It was Marcus Ratliff. Alex recognized him from the picture on his website.

The Stork opened a door that led to the basement. He gestured for Alex and Lara to walk down the stairs.

Stefan sat on a chair in the middle of the room. He was blindfolded, with his hands and ankles tied and a handkerchief stuffed in his mouth. A lump on his forehead above his left eye was caked in dried blood.

The Stork and the Snowman sat Alex and Lara down on two other chairs and then tied and gagged them. Car wheels crunched on the gravel driveway. A car door slammed and footsteps approached the house. *"Je Tomas,"* the Snowman said. *It's Tomas.* The Stork started to put a blindfold on Alex but the Snowman stopped him, saying something in Berovian that Alex didn't catch. The Stork nodded and removed the cloth from Stefan's eyes. Then the two men went upstairs.

Alex looked at his brother and then at Lara. He knew they were as scared as he was. Scared to death. Scared *of* death. The situation felt unreal, like a bad dream, but he knew it was no dream. He tried to think of a good reason why the Stork and the Snowman wouldn't kill them, desperate for something that would give him hope. Then he realized why they hadn't put blindfolds on him and Lara, and all hope vanished like a puff of smoke. He and Lara had seen the Snowman's new face. They would be able to give a description to the police. The Stork and the Snowman were not about to let that happen.

Alex looked around the room for something they could use to free themselves. The basement was unfinished. Smooth concrete walls and a concrete floor. Four smooth black metal poles supporting the plumbing pipes that ran along the ceiling. The three chairs they were sitting on.

It was hopeless.

Lara was gesturing with her head, directing him to look at something behind him. He shuffled his feet, moving his chair an inch at a time until he could see what she was looking at. All he could see was an old furnace. It was rounded and smooth. He looked back at Lara. She dipped her head toward the floor. He followed her gaze. A thin, curved foot that supported the furnace extended a few inches into the air at the end.

He inched his chair over to it until he was in the right position, then tipped himself over, keeping his head up so that it wouldn't hit the floor when he fell. He landed on his shoulder with a painful thump. He wiggled around until the rope between his wrists was against the metal foot and began sawing away. After a couple of minutes his shoulder muscles were screaming in agony but he ignored the pain. He worked away for what seemed like forever before he started to feel the rope give way. He sped up. The rope fibers broke, one by one, until he was finally free.

He was reaching down to untie the rope around his ankles when the door at the top of the stairs opened. He heard two sets of footsteps coming down the stairs and across the floor. A few seconds later he was staring at a pair of polished black shoes.

The Stork jerked Alex upright. Tomas was standing beside him. He looked at Alex and shook his head sadly, as if Alex had disappointed him. The two men dragged Alex's chair over to one of the metal poles supporting the plumbing pipes. They tied Alex's hands around the pole, and then did the same with Lara and Stefan.

Alex looked at Stefan. His eyes were closed. It was hard to tell if he was conscious. He turned to Lara. She had a frightened look on her face. It took all Alex's willpower not to look away. *I should never have let her come with me,* he thought.

After a while—Alex had no idea how long—the door opened again. He heard footsteps come down the stairs. *Was it going to happen now?* He felt like he was going to faint. *I don't want to die,* he silently screamed.

Tomas was carrying a tray with three bowls of soup. Alex felt a glimmer of hope. *They wouldn't feed us if they planned to kill us, would they?* Then he saw the sad look on Tomas's face and knew there would be no reprieve. Whatever he was, Tomas was no killer. He didn't want them to die. But it was out of his hands.

He took the gag out of Lara's mouth so he could feed her.

"I need to pee," she said.

Tomas untied her hands. He took the gun out of his waistband and stepped back while she undid the rope around her ankles.

Tomas pointed to the stairs. Lara walked unsteadily toward them. She reached out and grabbed the railing for support. When she stepped onto the second stair, she whirled around and booted the gun out of Tomas's hand with one leg and kicked him in the groin with the other. As he doubled over in pain, Lara grabbed his head with both hands and drove it down at the same time as she brought her knee up. Tomas sighed softly and sank to the floor.

Lara rushed over to Alex and untied his hands, and then went to free Stefan. Alex pulled the handkerchief out of his mouth and untied the ropes around his ankles before hurrying to help Lara with Stefan. His brother was pale. They helped him to his feet. His legs gave out. He would have fallen if they hadn't been there to catch him.

"Sit down," Alex said. They helped him back onto the chair.

"I'll be okay in a minute," Stefan said. He took one of the bowls of soup and hungrily drank some. It seemed to revive him a little.

Tomas groaned.

"We'd better tie him up," Lara said. She and Alex dragged Tomas over to one of the metal poles and tied and gagged him. Alex picked Tomas's gun off the floor and put it in his jacket pocket. It was heavier than he expected.

"Do you have your phone?" Alex asked. Stefan shook his head.

There were no windows in the basement. The only way out was up the stairs.

"Can you walk?" Alex asked. Stefan nodded. Alex helped him get to his feet and supported him as they slowly made their way up the stairs. When they got to the top, Alex took the gun out of his pocket. Lara turned the knob. The door opened soundlessly. They stepped into the hallway.

Marcus Ratliff stood in the kitchen with his back to them, arranging his surgical instruments on a tray beside the stretcher. Alex crept up behind him and put the gun up against the back of his head.

"One word and I blow your head off." It sounded like a line from a bad movie but it worked. "Get on the stretcher," he whispered. Ratliff lay down on the table, his eyes wide with fear. Alex kept the gun pointed at Ratliff while Lara tied and gagged him. Stefan leaned against the wall. He was in bad shape.

They could hear the murmured voices of the Stork and the Snowman coming from the living room.

"Loko sive?" one of them called out. *How much longer?*

Alex froze. He and Lara looked at each other helplessly.

Stefan came to the rescue. *"Pet minuta,"* he called out, coughing to disguise his voice. *Five minutes.* The three of them stood still, not even daring to take a breath until they heard the Stork and the Snowman resume their conversation.

Alex pointed to the back door. The three of them crept toward it. Alex slowly turned the knob and pulled. The door was locked with a double deadbolt. They would need the key to open it. Lara spotted a set of keys hanging on a hook by the door. There were five keys, including a black one with the Mercedes logo on it.

The first key Lara tried didn't work. She was about to try a second when they heard footsteps coming toward them. They hurried to the door to the hallway. Lara grabbed a wooden stool and hid on one side. Alex and Stefan hid on the other. Alex took the gun out of his jacket pocket. His hand was shaking.

A few seconds later the Snowman stepped into the kitchen. He saw Ratliff lying on the operating table. Before he could move, Lara smashed the stool down on his head from behind. He sank to his knees. Lara hit him with the stool again. The fat man crumpled to the floor.

"*Lok seder?*" the Stork called from the living room. *Is everything okay?*

"*Da,*" Stefan called back. *Yes.*

They rushed to the back door, Stefan leaning heavily on Alex. Lara tried another key. This one slid smoothly into the lock. Lara opened the door and pocketed the keys. They snuck outside. It was dark but there was enough moonlight for them to see where they were going. Alex put the gun back in his jacket pocket and half-carried Stefan as they made their way to the front of the cabin. Lara got behind the wheel of the Mercedes. Alex opened the passenger door and helped Stefan inside. He collapsed into the seat, pale as a ghost.

"Are you okay?" Alex whispered. Stefan didn't have the strength to answer.

"We have to get him to the hospital," Lara said.

She started the car. Alex closed Stefan's door and was about to get in the back when Lara yelled out a warning. Alex looked up and saw the Stork running toward him. He was only a few feet away. There was no time for Alex to get into the car. "Go," he shouted. He ran toward the woods. He heard Lara gun the engine. The car wheels spun on the gravel driveway and then sped away. He ran out of the woods and down the driveway, where the footing was better. He glanced over his shoulder. The Stork was chasing him, but he was losing ground. *I'm going to make it,* Alex thought.

He didn't see the tree branch lying across the driveway until it was too late.

The next thing he knew he was flying though the air. He stuck his hands out at the last moment to break his fall.

He quickly rolled onto his knees and took the gun out of his jacket pocket. As the Stork took a step toward him, Alex fired wildly. The gunshot missed the Stork but it was enough to stop him in his tracks.

Alex clambered to his feet. He pointed the gun at Zarkov. They both knew he wouldn't miss this time.

The Stork put his hands up in the air without asking. "Don't shoot," he said.

"On the ground," Alex shouted.

The Stork sank to his knees.

This was the moment Alex had dreamed about. The final scene of the movie he had fantasized about so often. Here he was, face-to-face with the man who had murdered his father, the man who had laughed while his father was being burned alive, the man who had torn his family apart. Every fiber in his body cried out for revenge. He couldn't have planned it any better. Out in the middle of nowhere with nobody else in sight. If the police asked questions, he would say it was self-defense. They could never prove it wasn't.

He cocked the trigger. He could see the look of fear on the Stork's face in the moonlight, and the Stork must have been able to see the look of grim determination on his.

"Don't shoot. Please don't shoot," he whimpered.

Alex extended his arm but he couldn't pull the trigger. "Lie face down on the ground," he said. "Put your hands out in front of you."

The Stork did as he was told.

Alex stood in the darkness, listening to the silence. It was finally broken by the wail of police sirens in the distance. Faint at first, but getting louder.

CHAPTER FORTY-THREE

"It almost feels like things are back to normal," Anna said as they were driving to the arena for the first game of the provincial championships. West Vancouver was playing the Prince Rupert Commodores.

The past week had been surreal.

The Stork and the Snowman were extradited to the Netherlands to stand trial for their crimes, and if they were convicted, a near certainty, they would spend the rest of their lives in prison. Tomas Radich, Marcus Ratliff, and Peter Jurak also faced lengthy prison sentences.

The arrest of the Stork and the Snowman was front-page news around the world. When the police first announced that three teenagers had captured the two war criminals, the story was treated as a hoax by a number of news organizations. The idea that three kids could succeed where Interpol had failed seemed preposterous. When it proved to be true, the media circled like a pack of vultures.

Interest in the story was so intense that Anna and Lara's parents hired a lawyer to handle the interview requests. The lawyer wisely announced that any news organization that contacted the kids without permission would be denied an interview, a strategy that kept the press at bay. They ultimately did a single interview with a reporter from CBC TV on the understanding that the footage would be made available to everyone else.

"You're sure you're feeling all right?" Anna asked Stefan. He was sitting beside her in the front seat. "No more double vision?"

"I'm fine," Stefan said.

"Why are your eyes closed?"

"I'm just trying to focus on the game and forget about everything else," Stefan said. Alex knew that couldn't be easy. Maybe Anna felt as though things were getting back to normal, but it sure didn't feel like it to him. Their lawyer had kept the news organizations at a distance, but the phone had rung off the hook with calls from people none of them had seen in years. Things had gotten so out of hand that everybody moved into a hotel under assumed names. School had been a zoo, as well. Even though all the details had been in the paper and on TV, everybody, even the teachers, wanted to get the story first-hand. Alex, Stefan, and Lara couldn't walk down the hallway without getting swarmed.

No, Alex thought, *things aren't quite back to normal.*

"I'll meet you right here after the game," Anna said as she pulled up in front of the entrance to the arena, "and then we'll go get Boris." Boris hadn't been able to fly out of Maldania until today due to a snowstorm that had shut down the airport in Grabel. Anna was on her way to the store in Abbotsford. The pipes had burst early that morning and she had to meet the insurance adjustor.

Alex and Stefan got out of the car. West Van was playing the first game of the tournament, and they had arrived a half hour before McAndrew had told the team to report, so the arena was quiet when they walked inside.

Alex hadn't given much thought to hockey in the three weeks since the season ended. There had been other things on his mind: the magical trip to Europe with Lara and then the incredible adventure that culminated in the capture of the Stork and the Snowman. But he started thinking about it as soon as he and Stefan stepped into the empty West Van locker room.

He wondered if he would ever play competitive hockey again. He was going to the University of British Columbia next year and he would try out for the team, but his odds of making it weren't good. The Thunderbirds weren't losing many players, and the recruits who had received scholarships had the inside track on the few positions that were available.

He thought of all the locker rooms he'd walked into over the years; he remembered the pre-game rush of anticipation mixed with fear and excitement, the feeling of being a warrior, of knowing that he would soon be put to the test. It saddened him to think that he might never experience that again. He thought about the disappointing way the season had ended after it had started with such high hopes. If his career was over, so be it, but he wished it hadn't ended like that, without having had the chance to put himself to the test one final time. He would have given anything for the opportunity to strap his pads on one more time, for the chance to scratch that itch and prove he still had it, even if it was only to himself.

Stefan tossed his hockey bag on the floor and sat down on a chair. He sighed heavily and put his head in his hands.

"Are you okay?"

"Not really."

"What's wrong?"

"I'm seeing double."

"What? You said you were fine."

"It started again this morning. I was hoping it would go

away."

"You have to tell McAndrew you can't play."

"We can't win with Dempster in goal. He sucks." Jack Dempster was the West Van backup goalie.

"Doesn't matter. You can't play if you're seeing double. You could get hurt."

"I know that."

"So there's no problem."

"No problem? It's the provincial championships."

"I know," Alex said, "but there's nothing you can do about it."

"You play for me."

"What?" Alex stared at his brother in disbelief.

"You play for me. You pretend you're me."

"Are you crazy?"

"Nobody will find out. It's just for one game. I'll be okay tomorrow."

"You're crazy." The idea was completely insane. He hadn't played in a real game in three months. And now his brother wanted him to play in the provincials. It was a ridiculous idea. Completely ridiculous. And all Alex could think about was how much he wanted to do it.

"Come on," Stefan said, reading his mind. "You know you want to."

"We'll never get away with it."

"Sure we will."

"This is insane," Alex said. "Why are you doing this?"

"Does it matter?" He gave Alex a challenging look.

Alex met his brother's gaze. Then he unzipped Stefan's hockey bag and took out his long underwear. "I hope you washed this stuff," he said.

Stefan took off the jacket and tie McAndrew had ordered the players to wear, put on Alex's street clothes, and walked out of the locker room.

A few minutes later, the West Van players started arriving.

"Hey, Stefan. How you feeling?"

Alex gave a thumbs-up.

"S'up Stefan? You good to go?"

Another thumbs-up.

Alex realized he didn't have to worry that his new teammates would find out he was an impostor. They expected to see Stefan in a Lightning jersey and that's what they saw. Fears that he would be outed were soon replaced by the usual pre-game jitters.

He put on his gear. Jock, underwear, pants, left skate, right skate, left pad, right pad, chest protector. And finally the West Vancouver jersey with number 33 on the back. Alex caught a glimpse of himself in the mirror. It felt weird to be wearing the jersey of the Cougars' longtime rival.

Everybody was dressed when Coach McAndrew arrived. He looked around the room, making eye contact with everyone. Alex met his gaze. There wasn't a glimmer of doubt about who he was in the coach's eyes.

"All right, boys," he said. "This is it. You know what to do. Now go out there and do it."

It might have been the shortest pep talk in history.

The players gathered in the middle of the room around the coach. "One. Two. Three," they all shouted. At the last second Alex remembered to shout "Lightning" and not "Cougars."

The reality of the situation hit him as soon as he stepped out onto the ice. Who did he think he was, trying to take Stefan's place? His brother was one of the top ten high school goalies in North America. He was the backup goalie for a rep team.

By the time he skated down to the Lightning goal and put on his Lou Roberts mask he knew the game was going to be a disaster. He should never have agreed to do it. The first warm-up shot from one of his teammates went right through his legs. So did the second. He bent down to adjust one of his pads. *Get it together*, he told himself. He waited for the Voice to tell him he was making the biggest mistake of his life, but the Voice was strangely silent, at least the one he was used to hearing. *You can do it, man. You don't have to be Stefan. You just have to be yourself.*

Alex took a deep breath. He stood up and tapped his pads with his stick to let his teammates know he was ready. *Stick on the ice. Square up to the shooter. Stand your ground.* He turned the shot away. *Stick on the ice. Square up to the shooter. Stand your ground.* He blocked the next shot. And the one after that. By the time the referee blew his whistle to start the game, Alex felt pretty calm. But he knew he wouldn't relax completely until he faced his first shot.

He didn't have to wait long.

Prince Rupert controlled the opening face-off and dumped the puck into the corner to the left of the goal. The West Van defenseman chased after it, closely followed by the Commodores' left-winger.

"Man on, man on," Alex yelled to let his teammate know he didn't have much time, using what he hoped would pass for a Berovian accent. The accent worked but the warning didn't help. The Prince Rupert player bounced the Lightning's defenseman off the puck and slapped it along the boards to his centerman, who made a perfect pass to a teammate moving into the slot. He whipped a shot that was headed for the upper shelf but Alex snaked out his glove and made the save.

"Way to go, Stefan," his teammates yelled.

Prince Rupert kept up the pressure for the next few minutes but Alex was steady as a rock, giving the West Van offence time to find its stride. The match turned into a seesaw affair, the momentum shifting from one team to the other and back again. Alex and his Prince Rupert counterpart were tested time and time again.

West Van opened the scoring early in the second period but the Commodores came back with the equalizer a few minutes later, a screened shot Alex had no chance to stop. At the end of the period the score was tied 1–1.

Alex went into the locker room and collapsed on his chair. He was dog-tired. The three weeks of inactivity were taking a toll. The intermission seemed to pass in the blink of an eye. It took all his strength just to get back on his feet when it was time to go out on the ice again.

"Keep it up, big guy," one of his teammates said as they left the locker room to begin the third period. "We'll get one for you."

The Lightning did just that. Four minutes into the period they scored the go-ahead goal. Prince Rupert responded to the challenge and turned up the pressure. Over and over again they swept in on goal, and each time Alex turned them away. He was in the zone. It felt like the game was being played in slow motion.

The 2–1 lead held up. When the game ended, the West Van players spilled over the bench and skated down to the goal to congratulate him. The crowd was on its feet, cheering. When Alex reached the West Van bench, he stopped and looked into the stands, searching for his brother.

Stefan was on his feet, pumping his fist in the air. Lara was standing beside him, waving furiously, a huge smile on her face. Alex saluted them with his mask and then stepped off the ice.

Coach McAndrew didn't give his players much time to celebrate. "Nice win, gentlemen, but we've still got a lot of work ahead of us. We play the winner of Kamloops–Coquitlam tomorrow at noon so I want everybody to go home, get some rest, have a good breakfast tomorrow, and show up ready to play."

Alex sat in his uniform for fifteen minutes before he had the strength to take it off. It wasn't a problem continuing the pretense that he was Stefan. His teammates didn't bat an eye at his one-syllable responses when they congratulated him on his amazing performance. They could see that he was completely spent.

Alex texted Stefan after he showered, as arranged, and then put on his jacket and tie and headed for the washroom. A minute later Stefan walked into the locker room.

"Hey, Alex," said the few West Van players who hadn't yet left.

Stefan nodded.

"Your brother was awesome, man."

Stefan nodded again. He went into the washroom and entered the stall next to the one Alex was in. They switched clothes and then returned to the locker room.

"See you guys tomorrow," Stefan said, picking up his hockey bag.

"Later."

Lara was waiting outside the locker room. So were Roman and his wife, Sophia.

"Great game," Roman said to Stefan. "You were magnificent."

"Fantastic," Sophia said.

"Thanks."

"I'm so glad you're feeling better," Roman said to Stefan.

"You don't know how upset he's been at what happened," Sophia said.

"Everything worked out, so it's all good," Stefan said.

Lara went up to Alex and gave him a big hug. "You were incredible," she whispered. "I'm so proud of you."

"Young love," Roman said to Sophia. "Can't stand to be apart for more than five minutes. Remember when we were like that?"

"No," she said with a smile. She gave Roman a kiss on the cheek. "Roman told me about what you're planning to do with the reward," she said. "I think that's wonderful. Simply wonderful."

Alex, Stefan, and Lara had decided to donate the $500,000 reward to a charitable organization that supported child victims of war.

"We gotta get going," Roman said. "Good luck tomorrow," he said to Stefan.

"Call me later," Lara said to Alex.

"Okay."

She gave him another hug before leaving with Roman and Sophia.

Stefan grabbed the hockey bag. He and Alex headed for the exit. Bill Henry was standing in the hallway, talking to a scout from the University of North Dakota. He walked up to them.

"Hey, guys," he said.

"Hey."

"Heck of a game," he said to Stefan. "Best performance I've seen in a long time. If I didn't know any better, I'd have thought it was Lou Roberts behind that mask."

"Thanks."

"If they don't treat you right in Denver, give us a call."

"Too bad he doesn't know who *was* behind the mask," Stefan said after Bill Henry rejoined his friend. He didn't have to finish the thought. Alex knew what his brother was thinking. He was thinking the same thing. If Bill Henry knew he had been in goal, Alex just might have gotten that scholarship to the University of Minnesota after all.

"Looks like you got it back," Stefan said.

"Got what back?"

"Your mojo."

"Looks like I did."

It was funny, Alex thought. It was one of the best games he'd ever played. And, except for him, Stefan, and Lara, nobody else in the world would ever know about it. The crazy thing was that he didn't really care.

Anna was waiting outside the arena. "Congratulations," Anna said to Stefan. "I heard you were fantastic." She looked to Alex for confirmation.

"He was incredible."

"And you're still feeling all right?" Anna asked Stefan anxiously.

"One hundred percent," Stefan said.

"Who wants to drive?" Anna asked.

"I do," Stefan said before Alex could speak up.

Anna tossed the keys to him. Fired them would be a better description. An overhead toss from a few feet away. Stefan snaked a hand out and snagged the keys as easily as if she'd handed them to him.

An amazing catch for someone with double vision, Alex thought. Impossible, in fact. "Nice catch," he said.

Stefan gave him a wink and then walked to the driver's

door.

"You must be proud of your brother," Anna said.

Alex met his brother's eyes over the roof of the car. "He's the greatest."

Anna beamed. She ruffled Alex's hair in appreciation of his expression of brotherly love. "Why is your hair wet?" she asked.

ACKNOWLEDGEMENTS

I would like to thank my wife, Claudette Jaiko, my daughter, Laura, and my mother, Lita-Rose, for their encouragement and support during the writing of this book. I would also like to thank Gordon Betcherman, Monique Marchildon, David Diamond, and Jake Onrot for reading the manuscript and providing invaluable feedback. Thanks also to my nephews, Nicolas and Zacharie, who gave me the inside scoop on minor hockey, and to Ben Gross, John Wilkie, and Jim Marinow for their assistance during the research of the book.

I would also like to thank my wonderful agent, Patricia Ocampo, at Transatlantic Agency. And very special thanks go to my editor, Lynne Missen, for her patience and insight, and to the rest of the team at Penguin Canada.

I would be delighted to hear from readers. Please feel free to contact me by email: mbetcherman@gmail.com

Also by Michael Betcherman

BREAKAWAY

A year ago, 16 year-old Nick Macklin had it all. He was an A student and a talented hockey player, with a beautiful girlfriend and the best dad in the world—a man who was not only there for him when his mom died, but was also a star player for the Vancouver Canucks.

Then the bottom fell out. His father was convicted of murder and sentenced to life in prison for a crime Nick is convinced he didn't commit. Angry and bitter, alienated from school and friends, Nick devotes himself to seeking justice for his father. Who framed him? And why?

But freeing his dad is not his biggest challenge. His obsession with proving his father's innocence threatens to ruin his own life. Can Nick put the pieces of the puzzle together—and save his dad and himself?

Shortlisted for The John Spray Mystery Award.

Turn the page to read the start of Breakaway

BREAKAWAY

CHAPTER ONE

Nick sat in the front row of the courtroom. His heart pounded as the judge turned toward the jury foreman. "Has the jury reached a verdict?" he asked.

The foreman stood up. "We have, Your Honor. We find the defendant, Steven Macklin, guilty of murder in the first degree."

Nick jumped to his feet. "No!" he screamed.

Nick woke with a start. But waking up didn't end the nightmare. It never did. Because he hadn't invented the scene in the courtroom; it had really happened. And Steven Macklin, the man who was convicted of murder, wasn't an imaginary character he'd dreamed up. He was Nick's father.

Nick swung his legs over the side of the bed. The sun streamed through a crack in the blinds. It should have been a welcome sight after the rainiest October in Vancouver history, but Nick didn't notice. His mind was still back in the courtroom, on that day eleven months ago when his life had fallen apart.

He and his father only had enough time for a quick goodbye after the verdict was announced. Nick tried not to cry but he couldn't help it. He buried his head in his dad's chest, hiding his tears, and held on until the guard tapped him on the shoulder and said it was time to go.

"I love you, Nick," his father whispered, his voice cracking with emotion. He gave his son a final squeeze, then stepped back and looked Nick in the eyes. "Be strong, son," he said, his voice once again firm and steady.

"But it's not fair, Dad. It's not fair," Nick cried. "You didn't do it."

"That's what we're going to prove," his dad said confidently, "and as soon as we do, I'll be back home."

But his dad still wasn't home and they were no closer to finding out who really killed Marty Albertson than they had been the day he went to jail. All Nick knew now was what he knew then; that his dad was an innocent man.

Nick's thoughts were interrupted by a knock on the door. "Time to get up, Nick, or you'll be late for school," Helen called out.

"I'm up," he shouted. He heard Helen's footsteps disappear down the hallway. He knew he shouldn't have yelled at her. He should be grateful that she and Al had taken him in. But it was hard to feel grateful about anything while his father was behind bars. Check that. It wasn't hard, it was impossible.

His dad first raised the subject of Nick's living arrangements during the trial. They were in the kitchen playing backgammon, as they had hundreds of times before. "We need to have a back-up plan in case we lose," his father said. "We're not going to lose," Nick replied. He rolled the dice and made his move. "Your turn."

The next time the subject came up, Nick didn't have the luxury of avoiding the conversation. They were in the visiting room at the prison, the day after the verdict came down. "Why can't I stay at home?" Nick asked.

"You're only sixteen," his dad said. "You're too young to live alone. Monique and Dennis want you to go live with them. I think it's a good idea."

Nick disagreed. Uncle Dennis was his mother's brother. Nick liked him and Aunt Monique well enough, although he hadn't seen much of them since they moved to

Ontario six years earlier, not long after his mother died. But there was no way—"no effing way" was how he put it at the time—he was going to leave Vancouver and live three thousand miles away from his father.

That left boarding school as the only alternative, and Nick was resigned to going there when Al and Helen Hawkins invited him to come live with them. Al was his father's agent. He'd signed Nick's dad up when he was playing junior hockey, negotiated his first contract with the Vancouver Canucks, and had represented him ever since.

Living with the Hawkins was a more attractive proposition than sharing a dormitory with a roomful of preppy kids, and Nick agreed to move in with them despite one major concern: If Al thought he had the right to act like he was Nick's father just because Nick was living in his house, the two of them were going to have a major problem.

It turned out to be a non-issue. All Al did was lay down a few ground rules. If Nick was going to be out later than midnight, he had to call to let them know where he was. He was expected to help out around the house when he was asked, and he had to be home for Sunday night dinner.

"Personally, I don't give a hoot," Al had said, staring at Nick solemnly, with no trace of the smile that usually appeared on his round face, "but it's important to Helen, so it's important to me."

Nick didn't have a problem with any of that. It wouldn't stop him from doing the only thing that mattered: finding out who really killed Marty Albertson, so his dad could come back home.

CHAPTER TWO

The sun had disappeared by the time Nick got off the bus. As he walked up the stairs to the school's main entrance, it started to rain.

McAndrew was standing in the foyer. "Mr. Macklin. To what do we owe the pleasure?" he asked sarcastically. Nick walked past him without a word.

McAndrew was the vice-principal, which was an unfortunate coincidence for Nick because he also happened to be the coach of the West Vancouver Lightning, the local rep hockey team that Nick had played for. Nick had been one of the team's best players, but he quit just before the playoffs the previous March when his father lost his appeal—his last chance to persuade the court he was innocent.

Without Nick in the lineup the Lightning had lost in the finals and McAndrew had been on his case ever since. If Nick was one minute late for school—and he was usually a lot later than that—McAndrew was sure to give him a detention. That meant he was spending a lot of time in the study hall after school—not that he did much studying there. Doing well in school stopped being a priority the moment his father went to prison. He had barely scraped through grade eleven last year, and this year things looked even worse.

"Tough love" was the way McAndrew described it, but Nick knew that love had nothing to do with it. If he had still been playing hockey, he could have shown up at noon every day and McAndrew wouldn't have said boo.

"I know it can't be easy for you to deal with the situation," McAndrew said when he summoned Nick to his office just after school started, "but it's my job to make sure you get an education and that's what I intend to do."

The *situation*. That was the word everybody used to refer to what had happened. His English teacher, Mr. Putnam, would call it a euphemism—a vague word used to describe something unpleasant to make it seem less real. Like the way people said his mother had "passed away" instead of just coming right out and saying she was dead and gone forever.

It was the same with his dad. Calling what happened to him the *situation* didn't change the fact that he was serving a life sentence in prison for a murder he didn't commit. And nobody, including McAndrew, had a goddamn clue what that felt like.

Nick glanced back at the foyer as he walked into math class. McAndrew was still standing there, staring at him.

At four o'clock Nick left the school after sleepwalking his way through another day of classes. The sun had broken through the clouds. Red, Biggie, and Ivan were down the street, waiting for the bus. Nick couldn't help feeling a little envious as he watched his former teammates joking with each other in their leather jackets with West Vancouver Lightning written on the back. He missed being part of the team, he couldn't deny it. It was like having a second family.

That's what his dad always said about playing with the Canucks, and it was why he stayed with them for his whole career, even though he could have made more money with another team. It drove Al Hawkins crazy. "At least pretend you're thinking about playing somewhere else," Al said the last time his father was up for a new contract. "You gotta give me something to work with. If they know you want to stay in Vancouver, they're not going to cough up the do-re-mi." Do-re-mi was Al's corny way of saying money.

His dad just sat there and smiled. "I'm making plenty of money as it is. I don't need more. Nick and I are happy here. Besides, the team has always treated me fairly." Nick didn't think his father would say that now. Even though there were two years left on his five-year guaranteed contract, the conviction gave the team the legal right to terminate their agreement, and they didn't hesitate to use it. That was his dad's reward for sixteen years of uninterrupted service. Al fought them as hard as he could, but legally they were within their rights, and there wasn't much sympathy for a convicted murderer in the court of public opinion.

Google came running up just as the bus arrived. Google, a.k.a. Mark Mandell, had played Atom, Peewee, and Bantam with the guys. When he didn't make the Midget team last year, he signed on as team manager. They called him Google because there wasn't anything about computers that he didn't know.

Nick watched his friends board the bus. The five of them used to be inseparable. If they weren't playing hockey, they were talking about it or watching it on TV. For a moment he imagined he was with them, talking strategy and psyching themselves up for the game, like they'd done so many times in the past.

But that was Before.

Before and After. His life was divided in two, just like world history was divided into BC and AD. But instead of Nick's reference point being the birth of Jesus Christ, it was the day his father had gone to jail.

Nick couldn't remember the last time he'd hung with the guys. It was his own doing. For months they kept calling, but he kept making excuses, and after a while, the phone stopped ringing.

Nick watched the bus pull away. The Lightning had a game against the Burnaby Owls, and his friends were headed to La Fortuna for the pre-game meal. The restaurant was owned by Red's parents and the guys ate there before every home game. Nick didn't know how many times he'd been at the restaurant, but there was one time he'd never forget. It had started out as one of the best days of his life and ended up being one of the worst.

It happened less than two years ago, even though it felt like a century. The Lightning had won the Bantam AA championship. Red's parents hosted a banquet at La Fortuna. Nick's dad couldn't come because the Canucks were playing.

After dinner, they all watched the Canucks' game on TV. It was the last game of the season. Vancouver had already qualified for the playoffs, but the Leafs needed a win or they were out. With a couple of minutes left, the Canucks were leading 3-0. There he was, surrounded by his best buddies, watching his father on TV. The Canucks were going to the playoffs, and the Leafs were going golfing. Life didn't get much sweeter than that.

Then it happened. "The hit."

Nick must have seen it a couple of hundred times in the days after it happened and then a couple of hundred more during the trial. His dad was skating across center ice when the Leafs' Marty Albertson raced up from behind and viciously cross-checked him on the head. His dad went down like he'd been shot. The image of him lying there, crumpled on the ice was seared into Nick's memory. His father was in a coma for a week. The doctors weren't sure if he would ever walk again. To their amazement he was back on his feet in two months, but there was no question of his ever playing hockey again.

Albertson was suspended for thirty games. Thirty measly games for one of the dirtiest hits in hockey history! The day the league made the announcement, a reporter for a local TV station asked Nick's dad for his reaction. Enraged, he said Albertson should have been thrown in jail and barred from hockey for life. Nick had never seen his father so angry.

Five months later Marty Albertson was dead, and Nick's dad was charged with his murder. At the trial his furious reaction to Albertson's suspension came back to haunt him. The Crown Attorney said it explained why he killed him. "You don't have to look very hard to find a motive in this case," he told the jury. "When the league didn't stop Marty Albertson from playing hockey, Steve Macklin decided to do it himself."

The case against his dad was simple enough. Albertson had played with the Canucks before he was traded to the Leafs, and he still lived in Vancouver during the off-season. On the morning of September 18, his body was found in his condo by a man he'd hired to paint the living room. Albertson was slumped in an armchair with one bullet in his head and another in his heart.

The autopsy report said he died sometime between four and seven the previous evening. When the police found an entry in Albertson's BlackBerry showing he had scheduled a meeting with Steve Macklin at five p.m. that day, they gave Nick's father a call.

Nick's dad told the police that Albertson called him around four p.m. and asked if they could meet to talk about what happened. The call came out of the blue. It was the first time they had spoken since "the hit." That was a real sore point with Nick's dad, especially since the two of them had been teammates before Albertson was traded to the Leafs. The Crown Attorney used that against him at the trial as well.

Nick's father said Albertson was supposed to come to their house in West Van at five p.m. but he never showed. He said he waited around until six-thirty, and then he left the house for a fundraising event at a hospital in downtown Vancouver.

The police didn't believe him. According to Albertson's BlackBerry, the meeting was to take place at his condo, not at the Macklin house in West Van. The police examined the clothes Nick's dad was wearing the night of the murder and found a small trace of beige paint on the back of his suit jacket, up near his shoulder. When tests proved the paint on his jacket matched the fresh paint in Albertson's living room, he was arrested.

At first Nick's dad couldn't explain how the paint ended up on his jacket. He claimed he'd never even been to Albertson's condo. Then he remembered that he had spoken to a man—a bald man—as he went into the washroom just before the fundraiser started. The man had approached him from behind, tapped him on his shoulder to get his attention, told him he was a big fan—and then limped away. Nick's dad said the bald man must have put the paint on his jacket when he tapped him on his shoulder.

The police didn't buy the explanation, and when the detectives Nick's dad hired couldn't find the bald man, neither did the jury.

Breakaway by Michael Betcherman

Made in the USA
Middletown, DE
22 June 2019